FORWARD/COMMENTARY

The National Institute of Standards and Technology (NIST) is a measurement standards laboratory, and a non-regulatory agency of the United States Department of Commerce. Its mission is to promote innovation and industrial competitiveness. Founded in 1901, as the National Bureau of Standards, NIST was formed with the mandate to provide standard weights and measures, and to serve as the national physical laboratory for the United States. With a world-class measurement and testing laboratory encompassing a wide range of areas of computer science, mathematics, statistics, and systems engineering, NIST's cybersecurity program supports its overall mission to promote U.S. innovation and industrial competitiveness by advancing measurement science, standards, and related technology through research and development in ways that enhance economic security and improve our quality of life.

The need for cybersecurity standards and best practices that address interoperability, usability and privacy has been shown to be critical for the nation. NIST's cybersecurity programs seek to enable greater development and application of practical, innovative security technologies and methodologies that enhance the country's ability to address current and future computer and information security challenges.

The cybersecurity publications produced by NIST cover a wide range of cybersecurity concepts that are carefully designed to work together to produce a holistic approach to cybersecurity primarily for government agencies and constitute the best practices used by industry. This holistic strategy to cybersecurity covers the gamut of security subjects from development of secure encryption standards for communication and storage of information while at rest to how best to recover from a cyber-attack.

Why buy a book you can download for free?

Some are available only in electronic media. Some online docs are missing pages or barely legible.

We at 4th Watch Books are former government employees, so we know how government employees actually use the standards. When a new standard is released, an engineer prints it out, punches holes and puts it in a 3-ring binder. While this is not a big deal for a 5 or 10-page document, many NIST documents are over 100 pages and printing a large document is a time-consuming effort. So, an engineer that's paid $75 an hour is spending hours simply printing out the tools needed to do the job. That's time that could be better spent doing engineering. We publish these documents so engineers can focus on what they were hired to do – engineering. It's much more cost-effective to just order the latest version from Amazon.com

If there is a standard you would like published, let us know. Our web site is Cybah.webplus.net

Please see the Cybersecurity Standards list at the end of this book.

CyberSecurity Standards Library™

Get a Complete Library of Over 300 Cybersecurity Standards on 1 Convenient DVD!

The **4th Watch CyberSecurity Standards Library** is a DVD disc that puts over 300 current and archived cybersecurity standards from NIST, DOD, DHS, CNSS and NERC at your fingertips! Many of these cybersecurity standards are hard to find and we included the current version and a previous version for many of them. The DVD includes four books written by Luis Ayala: **The Cyber Dictionary, Cybersecurity Standards, Cyber-Security Glossary of Building Hacks and Cyber-Attacks**, and **Cyber-Physical Attack Defenses: Preventing Damage to Buildings and Utilities**.

- ✓ DVD includes many Hard-to-find Cybersecurity Standards - some still in Draft.
- ✓ Docs are organized by source and listed numerically so each standard is easy to locate.
- ✓ The listing of standards on the DVD includes an abstract of the subject, and date issued.
- ✓ PDF format for use on PC, Mac, eReaders, or tablets.
- ✓ No need for WiFi / Internet.
- ✓ Save countless hours of searching and downloading.
- ✓ Carry in a briefcase - terrific for travel.

4th Watch Publishing is releasing the CyberSecurity Standards Library DVD to make it easier for you to access the tools you need to ensure the security of your computer networks and SCADA systems. We also publish many of these standards on demand so you don't need to waste valuable time searching for the latest version of a standard, printing hundreds of pages and punching holes so they can go in a three-ring binder. **Order on Amazon.com**

The DVD works on PC and Mac with the standards in PDF format. To view the CyberSecurity Standards Library on the DVD, a computer with a DVD drive is required. The most current version of your internet browser, at least 2GB of RAM, and current version of Adobe Reader is recommended. (Compatible browsers include Internet Explorer 8+, Mozilla Firefox 4+, Apple Safari 5+, Google Chrome 15+)

NISTIR 7823

Advanced Metering Infrastructure Smart Meter Upgradeability Test Framework

Michaela Iorga
Scott Shorter

This publication is available free of charge from:
http://dx.doi.org/10.6028/NIST.IR.7823

National Institute of
Standards and Technology
U.S. Department of Commerce

NISTIR 7823

Advanced Metering Infrastructure Smart Meter Upgradeability Test Framework

Michaela Iorga
Computer Security Division
Information Technology Laboratory
National Institute of Standards and Technology

Scott Shorter
Electrosoft Services, Inc.
Reston, Virginia

This publication is available free of charge from:
http://dx.doi.org/10.6028/NIST.IR.7823

March 2015

U.S. Department of Commerce
Penny Pritzker, Secretary

National Institute of Standards and Technology
Willie May, Acting Under Secretary Of Commerce for Standards and Technology and Acting Director

National Institute of Standards and Technology Interagency Report 7823
71 pages (March 2015)

This publication is available free of charge from:
http://dx.doi.org/10.6028/NIST.IR.7823

Comments on this publication may be submitted to:

National Institute of Standards and Technology
Attn: Computer Security Division, Information Technology Laboratory
100 Bureau Drive (Mail Stop 8930) Gaithersburg, MD 20899-8930
Email: nistir7823@nist.gov

Reports on Computer Systems Technology

The Information Technology Laboratory (ITL) at the National Institute of Standards and Technology (NIST) promotes the U.S. economy and public welfare by providing technical leadership for the Nation's measurement and standards infrastructure. ITL develops tests, test methods, reference data, proof of concept implementations, and technical analyses to advance the development and productive use of information technology. ITL's responsibilities include the development of management, administrative, technical, and physical standards and guidelines for the cost-effective security and privacy of other than national security-related information in Federal information systems.

Abstract

As electric utilities turn to Advanced Metering Infrastructures (AMIs) to promote the development and deployment of the Smart Grid, one aspect that can benefit from standardization is the upgradeability of Smart Meters. The National Electrical Manufacturers Association (NEMA) standard SG-AMI 1-2009, "Requirements for Smart Meter Upgradeability," describes functional and security requirements for the secure upgrade—both local and remote—of Smart Meters. This report describes conformance test requirements that may be used voluntarily by testers and/or test laboratories to determine whether Smart Meters and Upgrade Management Systems conform to the requirements of NEMA SG-AMI 1-2009. For each relevant requirement in NEMA SG-AMI 1-2009, the document identifies the information to be provided by the vendor to facilitate testing, and the high-level test procedures to be conducted by the tester/laboratory to determine conformance.

Keywords

Smart Grid; Advanced Metering Infrastructure; cybersecurity; firmware upgradeability; test framework; testing

ACKNOWLEDGMENTS

The authors, Michaela Iorga of the National Institute of Standards and Technology (NIST) and Scott Shorter of Electrosoft, wish to thank their colleagues who reviewed drafts of this document and contributed to its technical content. A special note of thanks goes to Jim Foti, Nelson Hastings, Marianne Swanson and Victoria Pillitteri of NIST, Greg Hollenbaugh of Electrosoft, Aaron Snyder of EnerNex Labs, and Isabelle Snyder and Nate Paul of Oak Ridge National Laboratory (ORNL) for their keen and insightful assistance throughout the development of the document. The authors also acknowledge and thank Elizabeth Lennon of NIST for her technical editing.

TABLE OF CONTENTS

LIST OF FIGURES

1. Introduction

1.1. Purpose

The United States has embarked on a major process of transforming the nation's electrical power grid into an advanced digital infrastructure with two-way capabilities for communicating information, controlling equipment, and distributing energy. Public and private efforts are focusing on formulating effective strategies for protecting the privacy of Smart Grid-related data and for securing the computing and communication networks that will be central to the performance, reliability, and security of the electric power infrastructure.

With the ongoing transition of the current electrical power grid to the Smart Grid, the information technology and telecommunication sectors will be more directly involved, and this cross-industry collaboration is expected to accelerate Smart Grid standards development. While other cybersecurity standards and specifications may address different functionality and security aspects of Smart Grid systems, this document is only proposing a voluntary test framework for the firmware upgradeability process of the Advanced Metering Infrastructure (AMI) Smart Meters. This test framework document aims to demonstrate the concept of assessing the Smart Meters' conformance to the National Electrical Manufacturers Association (NEMA) standard: NEMA SG-AMI 1-2009, "Requirements for Smart Meter Upgradeability."

Firmware upgrade is the process of installing new executable code onto a device; that code implements the functional capabilities of that device. Therefore, securely managing what code is installed on a device is of critical importance for securing a system. AMI systems are a particular case where devices (Smart Meters) and their network are deployed in physically insecure environments. This increased vulnerability enhances the need for a reliable and tested mechanism for security management functions such as the ability to query devices for their firmware versions and remotely install firmware updates. NEMA SG-AMI 1-2009 is a cybersecurity standard that was developed to address that need.

This document was developed with the purpose of identifying the **Functional Requirements** and describing the **Assurance Requirements** that may be used voluntarily by laboratories and/or testers to determine whether a Smart Meter conforms to NEMA SG-AMI 1-2009. Functional Requirements are those that pertain to the functionality of the Smart Meter or other item subject to conformance testing. Assurance Requirements are those that pertain to the method of assessment and testing used to ascertain whether the Functional Requirements have been met. Conformance tests applicable to Smart Meters are described in the following sections:

- Section 2, **Conformance Tests for Mandatory Requirements Applicable to Smart Meters;**
- Section 3, **Conformance Tests for Conditional Functional Requirements Applicable to Smart Meters;**
- Section 4, **Conformance Tests for Optional Functional Requirements Applicable to Smart Meters;**
- Section 5, **Non-testable Functional Requirements for Smart Meters;**
- Section 6, **Conformance Tests for Mandatory Functional Requirements for Upgrade Management Systems**.

It is important to note that Section 6 includes a requirement that mandates for the Upgrade Management Systems to meet same security requirements listed in Sections 3 and 5 for Smart Meters.

Several functional requirements from NEMA SG-AMI 1-2009 are outside the scope of this document. Those functional requirements comprise Sections 3.3, 3.4, and 3.5 of the NEMA Standard ("Metrology," "AMI Applications and Communications," and "HAN[1] Applications and Communications," respectively). Section 3.3 of the standard contains two requirements (3.3.1 and 3.3.2) and a statement (3.3.3) that is not mandatory and untestable. Notably, requirements 3.3.1 and 3.3.2 for Metrology are similar to the Smart Meter requirements 3.2.6 and 3.2.8, respectively addressed in Section 2 below by FR.NEMA-6 and FR.NEMA-8.

The **Assurance Requirements** that the vendor and tester need to fulfill during the testing process in order to show system's conformance with this standard are grouped in two categories:

- **Required Vendor Information:** assurance requirements levied on the vendor, and
- **Required Test Procedures:** assurance requirements levied on the tester.

The **Required Vendor Information** consists of documentation to be provided to users and/or the testing laboratory. This documentation shall explain how the Smart Meter satisfies the requirements. The **Required Test Procedures** contain descriptions of the test cases to be fulfilled in order to demonstrate the correct implementation of the Functional Requirements; and are intended to provide objectivity and repeatability of the test process and ensure a consistent method for assessing compliance with NEMA SG-AMI 1-2009. The NEMA standard does not address specific details of interfaces, commands, or protocols to achieve a firmware upgrade, nor does it specify how the functional and security requirements contained in the specification are to be implemented. Required Test Procedures describe testing at a high level, and provide more detailed Test Steps for conducting the test and Test Results and Records for assessing and reporting on results of the test. This level of detail ensures that test methodology and reporting are consistent among users of this test framework.

1.2. Audience

The audience for this document includes numerous stakeholders in the Smart Grid space, particularly Smart Meter manufacturers, certifying bodies, accrediting bodies, test laboratories, and standards development organizations.

1.3. Scope

The Required Test Procedures in this document are applicable to Smart Meters that claim conformance to the NEMA Smart Grid Standards Publication SG-AMI 1-2009, "Requirements for Smart Meter Upgradeability." That document is referred to herein as "the Standard."

1.4. Approach

This document comprises several lists of Functional Requirements from the Standard, namely

- **Mandatory Functional Requirements:** these requirements shall be demonstrated in order for a Smart Meter and/or Upgrade Management System to pass testing for conformance to the Standard;
- **Conditional Functional Requirements:** these requirements do not apply to all Smart Meters, but conformance to these requirements shall be demonstrated if the Smart Meter supports certain functionality or has certain properties; and

---

[1] **HAN**—Home Area Network - For the purpose of this document, HAN includes residential, commercial, and industrial services.

- **Optional Functional Requirements:** conformance with these requirements is recommended to be demonstrated, but not mandated.

1.5. Introduction to Conformance Testing

The NEMA Smart Grid Standards Publication SG-AMI 1-2009, "Requirements for Smart Meter Upgradeability," was published by the National Electrical Manufacturers Association in 2009. The purpose of the document is to define requirements for Smart Meter firmware upgradeability in the context of an AMI system for industry stakeholders such as regulators, utilities, and vendors.

The Conformance Test Requirements contained in this document have been derived from the Standard, and they consist of Functional Requirements and Assurance Requirements. These requirements are all mandatory for Smart Meters that claim conformance to the Standard.

If a certifying body such as a test laboratory or an entity assuming this role uses this test framework within an assessment and authorization (A&A) or certification scheme, the certification body becomes responsible for adopting, updating, or tailoring, when necessary, the test procedures described in this document and may choose to augment their A&A scheme with any suitable additional test procedures. Additionally, the certifying body has the right and responsibility to decide what tests may be performed by vendors (in-house testing), what tests may be performed by other parties external to the testing laboratory, and what tests are recognized only when performed by an accredited, third-party, testing laboratory.

As detailed above, **Functional Requirements** are specific requirements upon the Smart Meter, taken directly from the Standard. The Standard has separate sections for Functional Requirements and Security Requirements; the Functional Requirements in this document are drawn from both of those sections of the Standard. Some of the Functional Requirements are not applicable to Smart Meter conformance testing because they apply to the overall design of the AMI System or to components beyond the scope of control of the Smart Meter; some Functional Requirements are not presently testable due to wording in the Standard.

For each testable Functional Requirement applicable to Smart Meters, this document provides Assurance Requirements in the form of Required Vendor Information and Required Test Procedures. All **Functional Requirements** are denoted by the following abbreviated form

FR.NEMA-X[a]

where "X" is the sequence number of the Functional Requirement in the Standard and in this document. "X" may optionally be followed by a letter, indicating a sub-requirement that has been allocated to a different group of Functional Requirements (see FR-NEMA.2-5 and FR-NEMA.2-5a, for example). Each Functional Requirement is presented with its abbreviated form, a short title, and a reference to the corresponding requirement in the Standard. The text of the requirement from the Standard follows in italics, followed by a conditionality statement that explains whether a functional requirement is mandatory, conditional, or optional. Conditional requirements are mandatory if certain conditions are met; the conditionality statement identifies those conditions.

Required Vendor Information is information required to be documented by the manufacturer, vendor, or other sponsor of the testing. Required Vendor Information supports the claim that the Smart Meter is designed to correctly implement the associated Functional Requirement so system administrators and operators will have sufficient information available to perform the relevant function and testers have sufficient information to conduct testing. The requirements specify what information is required but not the format of that information. Required Vendor Information may be satisfied by data files in some cases (e.g., if configuration needs to be captured or an induced-failure firmware images for testing). Required Vendor Information produced during the test process should be protected in accordance with the agreement between the vendor and the tester. This Required Vendor Information is denoted by the form

RVI.NEMA-X.Y

where "X" corresponds to the Functional Requirement that this Required Vendor Information supports, and "Y" is the sequence number of the Required Vendor Information item for that Functional Requirement.

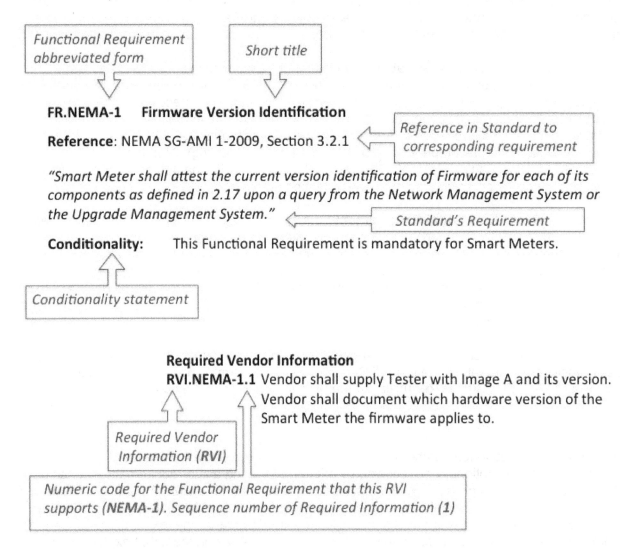

Required Test Procedures identify the determinations a tester shall make to verify the correct behavior of the Smart Meter. They are intended to be objective and repeatable, stated in a high-level and implementation-independent format. Required Test Procedures shall indicate what steps the tester should perform and what results are expected. During test preparation, testers derive implementation-specific test methods from the Required Test Procedures. These Required Test Procedures (RTP) are denoted by the form:

RTP.NEMA-X.Y

where "X" corresponds to the Functional Requirement for which this Required Test Procedure provides assurance, and "Y" is the sequence number of the Required Test Procedure for that Functional Requirement.

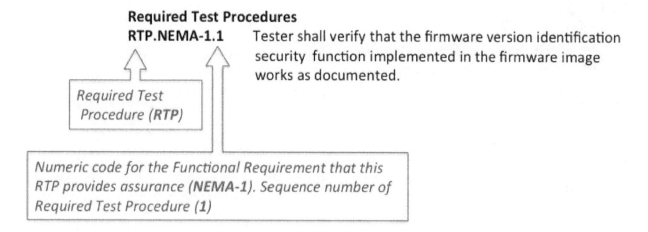

Following each Required Test Procedure are the high-level Test Steps that a tester shall follow in order to determine the Smart Meter's conformance to the particular Functional Requirement. Also included are the Test Records and Results that specify the assessment method for that test along with the information a tester shall record.

1.6. Conditionality and Applicability

1.6.1. Conditionality

The majority of the Functional Requirements in the Standard are clearly indicated as mandatory by the use of the verb "shall." In some cases, a mandatory requirement can be satisfied by one of a few choices of requirements—these are defined in this document as conditional requirements. Optional requirements are indicated by the verbs "may" or "should." Table 1 that summarizes the functional requirements, also indicates whether the requirement is mandatory (M), conditional (C) (and what conditions it depends on), or optional (O).

1.6.2. Applicability

This test framework was developed for the purpose of enabling testing of Smart Meters and their Upgrade Management Systems (UMS), and functional requirements for both are presented below. The target of the testing may be a Smart Meter, an Upgrade Management System, or both. Table 1 also identifies whether the Functional Requirements apply to the Smart Meter or the Upgrade Management System.

Table 1 - Functional Requirements – Conditionality and Applicability

Functional Requirement	Conditionality	Applies to Smart Meter	Applies to UMS
FR.NEMA-1	M	Y	N
FR.NEMA-2	M	Y	N
FR.NEMA-2a	C	Y	N
FR.NEMA-2b	C	Y	N
FR.NEMA-2c	O	Y	N
FR.NEMA-3	M	Y	N
FR.NEMA-4	M	Y	N
FR.NEMA-5	M	Y	(Y)
FR.NEMA-6	M	Y	N
FR.NEMA-7	M	Y	N
FR.NEMA-8	M	Y	N
FR.NEMA-9	M	Y	Y
FR.NEMA.10	M	Y	(Y)
FR.NEMA-11	M	Y	N
FR.NEMA-12	M	Y	(Y)
FR.NEMA-13	M	Y	(Y)
FR.NEMA-14	M	Y	(Y)
FR.NEMA-15	M	Y	(Y)
FR.NEMA-16	M	Y	(Y)
FR.NEMA-17	N	N	N
FR.NEMA-18	M	Y	(Y)
FR.NEMA-19	M	Y	(Y)
FR.NEMA-20	M	Y	(Y)
FR.NEMA-21	M	Y	(Y)
FR.NEMA-22	M	N	Y
FR.NEMA-23	M	N	Y
FR.NEMA-24	M	N	Y
FR.NEMA-25	M	N	Y

NOTE: The requirements marked with (Y) are implicitly mandated through the requirement FR.NEMA-24.

1.7. Test System Setup

Figure 1 below shows an abstract model of a test system setup that includes the following components:

- The Upgrade Management System (UMS)[2] – that represents any back-end components required to manage the upgrade process;
- The Test Application (TA) – that hosts any custom applications used to execute the tests; and
- The Smart Meter (SM)[3] – that receives the firmware upgrades, and which incorporates the Metrology[4] components and Communications Modules.[5]

---

[2] **Upgrade Management System**—"The hardware and software used to communicate and manage the Upgrade Process. The Upgrade Management System may be included in the Network Management System." [NEMA]

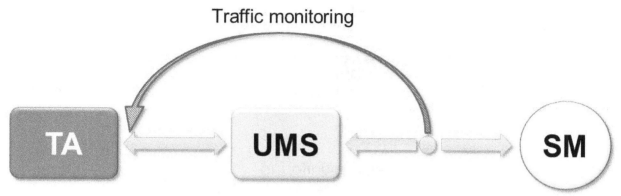

Figure 1 - Test System Setup

As a prerequisite for testing, the tester shall install and configure all test system components, establish communications between components, and create any accounts (administrator, device, and/or operator) that will be required for the tests. The vendor shall supply all of the Required Vendor Information listed below.

Ideally, Smart Meters and Upgrade Management Systems would be tested independently for conformance to the Standard. Such approach supports the testing of interoperable components that each fulfill their requirements according to the standard. This test framework therefore supports test scenarios in which the Smart Meter or the Upgrade Management System being evaluated is tested against a previously tested version of the other system component, referred to as a "gold" component. For example, a new Smart Meter can be tested with a "gold" Upgrade Management System (Figure 2), or a new UMS can be tested with a "gold" Smart Meter (Figure 3). There are a number of scenarios induced by either a particular architecture of the system, the unavailability of gold components[6], or by particular limitations of the capabilities offered by the testing laboratories, in which the Smart Meter and Upgrade Management Systems cannot be logically and/or physically isolated, and therefore tested as separate components. Such scenarios call for the Smart Meter and Upgrade Management System to be tested together. In these cases, the test approach assumes that no functionality has been previously tested and validated and therefore no Gold component exists for this testing purpose. Furthermore, the Smart Meter and the Upgrade Management System tested together cannot be used post testing in isolation from each other if the system's conformance is desired. The tests that fall under this category are gathered in Annex A.

---

[3] **Smart Meter**—"A device that includes Metrology, Communications Module, and, optionally, HAN interface. These components are typically integrated into a single physical unit suitable for installation in a standard utility meter socket. Sub-components may or may not be integrated on the printed circuit boards contained within the Smart Meter." [NEMA]

[4] **Metrology**—"The sub-component of a Smart Meter responsible for measuring and calculating Metered Data that may be used for register readings, time-of-use readings, load profile data, and other electrical or revenue measurement purposes. The Metrology may or may not be a separate electronic element and may or may not include other electronic elements or interfaces as well." [NEMA]

[5] **Communications Module**—"The sub-component of a Smart Meter responsible for AMI communications between Smart Meters in the field and the Network Management System. The Communications Module may or may not be a separate electronic element, and/or may include the HAN Interface." [NEMA]

[6] Gold component refers to a previously tested version of a system component, or to a validated or trusted prototype implementation.

When Gold components are available and the Smart Meters and/or Upgrade Management Systems can be logically and/or physically isolated, then testing laboratory shall proceed with individual testing of the components.

Smart Meter testing is applicable to the hardware version that is tested, and changes to the hardware version will require partial or full retesting. In addition to the information to be recorded for specific tests, the testing laboratory shall record the hardware version tested, and bind the hardware version to the tests performed.

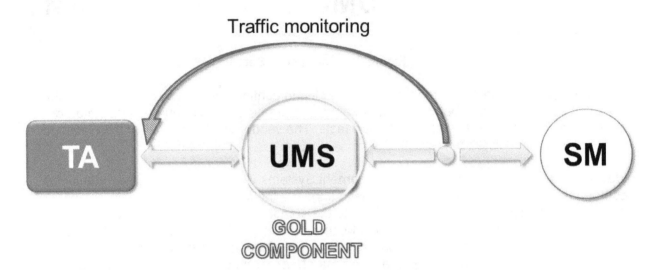

Figure 2 - Test System Setup for a Smart Meter

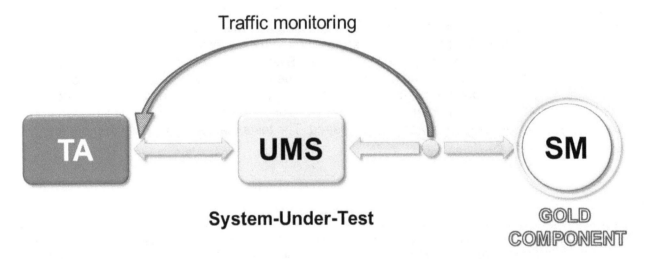

Figure 3 - Test System Setup for an Upgrade Management System

Until "gold" Smart Meters or Upgrade Management Systems are available, it is necessary to test both of them together as a system. Furthermore, at the time this test framework is written, there is no standardized communication protocol between the Upgrade Management Systems and Smart Meters, and testing these two components independently is not possible without developing customized tests for each component under test. Annex A provides a test scenario in which the Upgrade Management System and the Smart Meter are provisioned by the same vendor and are

8

tested for conformance as a single component under test. Because the Smart Meter and the Upgrade Management System are tested as a single component under test, some of the NEMA Upgradeability standard requirements cannot be tested. For more information, see Annex A.

Note that the Required Vendor Information refers in a number of places to firmware images to be provided to the Tester. The images are referenced by a letter or a letter and number code, and the same images may be used for different tests. To summarize, the images are:

- Image A – the "pre-upgrade" image, over which the new image will be installed. This may be the image installed on the Smart Meter when the Smart Meter is delivered to the Tester. The default initial state for testing a Functional Requirement is for Image A to be installed on the Test Smart Meter;
- Image B – the upgrade image to be installed over Image A;
- Image C – a corrupted image generated to test the firmware integrity check mechanism; and
- Images D1, D2, D3 – untrusted images, signed by untrusted certificates, expired certificates, and revoked certificates, respectively.

Because the functional requirements of the Smart Meter are largely implemented in firmware, care shall be paid to the specific versions of firmware used during tests. Whenever a firmware image is identified in test steps, the tester shall record the specific version used in the record for that test. Image A is the initial state for testing, and therefore the tests demonstrate whether Image A implements the security requirements correctly. For that reason, the test results are considered applicable to Image A.

2. Conformance Tests for Mandatory Requirements Applicable to Smart Meters

The mandatory Functional Requirements and associated Required Vendor Information and Required Test Procedures for Smart Meters are listed beneath.

FR.NEMA-1   Firmware Version Identification

Reference: NEMA SG-AMI 1-2009, Section 3.2.1

"Smart Meter shall attest the current version identification of Firmware for each of its components as defined in 2.17 upon a query from the Network Management System[7] or the Upgrade Management System."

Conditionality: This Functional Requirement is mandatory for Smart Meters.

Required Vendor Information

RVI.NEMA-1.1   Vendor shall supply Tester with Image A and its version. Vendor shall document which hardware version of the Smart Meter the firmware applies to.

RVI.NEMA-1.2   Vendor shall document the operations of the firmware version identification method.

Required Test Procedures

RTP.NEMA-1.1   Tester shall verify that the firmware version identification security function implemented in the firmware image works as documented.

Test Steps

1. Tester shall install Image A supplied by the Vendor in response to RVI.NEMA-1.1 on a Test Smart Meter.

2. Tester shall invoke the firmware version identification method as documented by the Vendor in response to RVI.NEMA-1.2 and record the version returned.

3. Tester shall confirm the firmware version identification security function worked as documented.

4. Tester shall confirm that the version returned by the Smart Meter matches the version claimed by the Vendor.

Test Results and Records

1. Tester shall record all Required Vendor Information that was used for the test. Tester shall document the hardware version of the Smart Meter tested.

2. Tester shall record all messages, responses, and event log records created during the test.

---

[7] **Network Management System**—"The system that controls and schedules communication on the AMI network, receives and stores information from Smart Meters and HAN devices, and sends information, including upgrade information, to devices on the network." [NEMA]

3. The test passes if all Test Steps complete successfully and Tester was able to positively confirm steps 3 and 4.

FR.NEMA-2   Firmware Upgrade Recovery

Reference: NEMA SG-AMI 1-2009, Section 3.2.2

"Smart Meter shall recover to the previously installed Firmware or initiate a "Failed Upgrade Process" alarm to the Network Management System or the Upgrade Management System if unable to complete the Upgrade Process."

Conditionality: This Functional Requirement is mandatory for Smart Meters.

Required Vendor Information

RVI.NEMA-2.1   Vendor shall document whether the Smart Meter recovers to previously installed firmware or initiates a "Failed Upgrade Process" alarm. If the Smart Meter recovers to previously installed firmware, the Conditional Functional Requirement FR.NEMA-2a is required. If the Smart Meter initiates a "Failed Upgrade Process" alarm, the Conditional Functional Requirement FR.NEMA-2b is required.

RVI.NEMA-2.2   Vendor shall document how the Smart Meter detects a failed Upgrade Process, and what actions are taken in response.

RVI.NEMA-2.3   Vendor shall supply Tester with two firmware images, Image A to be present on the Smart Meter before the upgrade, and Image B to be installed during the upgrade.

Required Test Procedures

RTP-NEMA-2.1   Based on the Vendor's response to RVI.NEMA-2.1, the Tester shall verify that the Smart Meter either recovers to previously installed firmware or initiates a "Failed Upgrade Process" alarm.

Test Steps

1. Tester shall review the Vendor's response to RVI.NEMA-2.1 and determine how the Smart Meter responds to being unable to complete the upgrade process.

2. Tester shall confirm that the responses include either a recovery to previously installed firmware or initiation of a "Failed Upgrade Process" alarm (or both).

Test Results and Records

1. Tester shall record all Required Vendor Information that was used for the test.

2. The test passes if all Test Steps complete successfully and Tester was able to positively confirm test step 2 (see above).

RTP-NEMA-2.2   Based on the Vendor's response to RVI.NEMA-2.1, the Tester shall execute the Required Test Procedures for the Conditional Functional Requirement FR.NEMA-2a and/or FR.NEMA-2b.

FR.NEMA-3   Firmware Completeness Validation

Reference: NEMA SG-AMI 1-2009, Section 3.2.3

"Smart Meter shall validate that Firmware Image reception is complete before effecting upgrade."

Conditionality: This Functional Requirement is mandatory for Smart Meters.

Required Vendor Information

RVI.NEMA-3.1   End-user guidance documents shall detail how to perform a firmware upgrade.

RVI.NEMA-3.2   Vendor shall document how the Smart Meter detects an incomplete firmware reception.

RVI.NEMA-3.3   Vendor shall document the Smart Meter's response to an incomplete firmware reception.

RVI.NEMA-3.4   Vendor shall supply Tester with two firmware images, Image A to be present on the Smart Meter before the upgrade, and Image B to be installed during the upgrade. The response to RVI.NEMA-2.3 may satisfy this requirement.

Required Test Procedures

RTP.NEMA-3.1   Tester shall conduct a successful firmware upgrade according to the methods in the Vendor's response to RVI.NEMA-3.1. This is the positive test case for the firmware upgrade process.

Test Steps

1. Tester shall install Image A on a Test Smart Meter.

2. Tester shall follow the methods in the Vendor's response to RVI.NEMA-3.1 to install Image B on the Test Smart Meter.

3. Tester shall invoke the firmware version identification function documented in the Vendor's response to RVI.NEMA-1.2 and record the version returned by the Test Smart Meter.

4. Tester shall confirm that the version returned matches the version for Image B.

Test Results and Records

1. Tester shall record all Required Vendor Information that was used for the test.

2. Tester shall record all messages, responses, and event log records created during the test.

3. The test passes if all Test Steps complete successfully and Tester was able to positively confirm step 4.

RTP.NEMA-3.2   Tester shall initiate an incomplete firmware upgrade process by disrupting the reception of the image B, and verify that the upgrade does not take effect and that the responses documented in the Vendor's response to RVI.NEMA-3.3 take place.

Test Steps

1. Tester shall install Image A on a Test Smart Meter.

2. Tester shall follow the methods in the Vendor's response to RVI.NEMA-3.1 to initiate installation of Image B on the Test Smart Meter.

3. Tester shall interfere with delivery of the complete Image B, disrupting it.

4. Tester shall confirm that the Smart Meter detects the incomplete image as described in the Vendor's response to RVI.NEMA-3.2.

5. Tester shall confirm that the Smart Meter responds as described in the Vendor's response to RVI.NEMA-3.3 when detecting the incomplete image.

6. If Vendor's response to RVI.NEMA-3.3 lists any of the operations identified in functional requirement FR.NEMA-2, tester shall confirm that the Smart Meter passes FR.NEMA-2.

Test Results and Records

1. Tester shall record all Required Vendor Information that was used for the test.

2. Tester shall record all messages, responses, and event log records created during the test.

3. The test passes if all Test Steps complete successfully and Tester was able to positively confirm steps 3 and 5.

FR.NEMA-4   Firmware Integrity Validation

Reference: NEMA SG-AMI 1-2009, Section 3.2.4

"Smart Meter shall validate that a Firmware Image passes Integrity Check before effecting upgrade."

Conditionality: This Functional Requirement is mandatory for Smart Meters.

Required Vendor Information

RVI.NEMA-4.1   Vendor shall document how the Smart Meter performs integrity check on firmware.

RVI.NEMA-4.2   Vendor shall document the Smart Meter's response to an integrity check failure.

RVI.NEMA-4.3   Vendor shall provide any necessary tools to enable the Tester to send a firmware image with compromised integrity. If the UMS normally detects integrity errors and does not send the image, then an additional test tool may be required to test the mechanism implemented by the Smart Meter that validates the integrity check verification.

RVI.NEMA-4.4   Vendor shall supply Tester with two firmware images, Image A to be present on the Smart Meter before the upgrade, and Image B to be installed during the upgrade. The response to RVI.NEMA-2.3 may satisfy this requirement.

Required Test Procedures

RTP.NEMA-4.1   This is the positive test case for the firmware upgrade integrity check process. This test is satisfied by completion of RTP.NEMA-3.1.

RTP.NEMA-4.2   Tester shall initiate a firmware upgrade process with an integrity check firmware error and verify that the upgrade does not take effect and that the responses documented in the Vendor's response to RVI.NEMA-4.2 take place.

Test Steps

1. Tester shall install Image A on a Test Smart Meter.

2. Based on the Vendor's response to RVI.NEMA-4.1, Tester shall modify the fields that implement the integrity mechanism for Image B, creating the corrupted Image C.

3. Tester shall follow the methods in the Vendor's response to RVI.NEMA-3.1 to attempt to install Image C on the Test Smart Meter.

4. Tester shall confirm that the Smart Meter responds as documented in the Vendor's response to RVI.NEMA-4.2.

5. If Vendor's response to RVI.NEMA-4.2 lists any of the operations identified in functional requirement FR.NEMA-2, tester shall confirm that the Smart Meter passes FR.NEMA-2.

Test Results and Records

1. Tester shall record all Required Vendor Information that was used for the test.

2. Tester shall record all messages, responses, and event log records created during the test.

3. The test passes if all Test Steps complete successfully and Tester was able to positively confirm steps 4 and 5.

FR.NEMA-5   Log Firmware Upgrade Attempts and Results

Reference: NEMA SG-AMI 1-2009, Section 3.2.5

"Smart Meter Upgrade Process attempts and results shall be logged."

Conditionality: This Functional Requirement is mandatory for Smart Meters.

Required Vendor Information

RVI.NEMA-5.1   Vendor shall document how the Smart Meter logs Firmware Upgrade attempts and results.

RVI.NEMA-5.2   Vendor shall supply Tester with two firmware images, Image A to be present on the Smart Meter before the upgrade, and Image B to be installed during the upgrade. The response to RVI.NEMA-2.3 may satisfy this requirement.

Required Test Procedures

RTP.NEMA-5.1   Tester shall perform a successful firmware upgrade process and verify that the upgrade attempt and successful results are logged. This test may be satisfied by gathering the log information during a positive test case such as RTP.NEMA-3.1.

Test Steps

1. Tester shall install Image A on a Test Smart Meter.

2. Tester shall follow the methods in the Vendor's response to RVI.NEMA-3.1 to install Image B on the Test Smart Meter.

3. Based on the Vendor's response to RVI.NEMA-5.1, Tester shall confirm that the Firmware Upgrade attempt was logged.

Test Results and Records

1. Tester shall record all Required Vendor Information that was used for the test.

2. Tester shall record all messages, responses, and event log records created during the test.

3. The test passes if all Test Steps complete successfully and Tester was able to positively confirm step 3.

RTP.NEMA-5.2   For each negative test case involving an induced failure elsewhere in this document, Tester shall initiate a failed firmware upgrade process and verify that the upgrade attempt and unsuccessful results are logged.

Test Steps

1. Tester shall install Image A on a Test Smart Meter.

2. Tester shall follow the methods in the Vendor's response to RVI.NEMA-3.1 to initiate installation of Image B on the Test Smart Meter.

3. Tester shall interfere with delivery of the complete image B, disrupting it.

4. Based on the Vendor's response to RVI.NEMA-5.1, Tester shall confirm that the Firmware Upgrade attempt was logged, with the failed results recorded.

5. Tester shall install Image A on a Test Smart Meter.

6. Based on the Vendor's response to RVI.NEMA-4.1, Tester shall modify the fields that implement the integrity mechanism for Image B, creating the corrupted Image C.

7. Tester shall follow the methods in the Vendor's response to RVI.NEMA-3.1 to attempt to install Image C on the Test Smart Meter.

8. Based on the Vendor's response to RVI.NEMA-5.1, Tester shall confirm that the Firmware Upgrade attempt was logged, with the failed results recorded.

Test Results and Records

1. Tester shall record all Required Vendor Information that was used for the test.

2. Tester shall record all messages, responses, and event log records created during the test.

3. The test passes if all Test Steps complete successfully and Tester was able to positively confirm steps 4 and 8.

FR.NEMA-6   No Metrology Recalibration

Reference: NEMA SG-AMI 1-2009, Section 3.2.6

"Smart Meter shall not require Metrology recalibration after Firmware upgrade."

Conditionality: This Functional Requirement is mandatory for Smart Meters.

Required Vendor Information

RVI.NEMA-6.1   Vendor shall document how to determine whether a Smart Meter requires Metrology recalibration. One way of determining if recalibration is necessary is an accuracy test performed at various loads to confirm that readings remain within the specified meter class range. A WECO device is an example of calibration device that may be used.

RVI.NEMA-6.2   Vendor shall supply Tester with two firmware images, Image A to be present on the Smart Meter before the upgrade, and Image B to be installed during the upgrade. The response to RVI.NEMA-2.3 may satisfy this requirement.

Required Test Procedures

RTP.NEMA-6.1   Tester shall perform a successful firmware upgrade process as documented in RTP.NEMA-3.1 and follow the methods documented in the Vendor's response to RVI.NEMA-6.1 to verify that the Smart Meter does not require Metrology recalibration.

Test Steps

1. Tester shall install Image A on a Test Smart Meter.

2. Tester shall follow the methods in the Vendor's response to RVI.NEMA-3.1 to install Image B on the Test Smart Meter.

3. Based on the Vendor's response to RVI.NEMA-6.1, Tester shall verify that the Smart Meter does not require Metrology recalibration.

Test Results and Records

1. Tester shall record all Required Vendor Information that was used for the test.

2. Tester shall record all messages, responses, and event log records created during the test.

3. The test passes if all Test Steps complete successfully and Tester was able to positively confirm step 4.

16

FR.NEMA-7   Configuration Persistence

Reference: NEMA SG-AMI 1-2009, Section 3.2.7

"Smart Meter shall support persisting existing Configuration after Firmware upgrade."

Conditionality: This Functional Requirement is mandatory for Smart Meters.

Required Vendor Information

RVI.NEMA-7.1   Vendor shall document how to configure a Smart Meter to persist the configuration after a firmware upgrade.

RVI.NEMA-7.2   Vendor shall document how to review and when possible how to export a Smart Meter's configuration.

RVI.NEMA-7.3   Vendor shall supply Tester with two firmware images, Image A to be present on the Smart Meter before the upgrade, and Image B to be installed during the upgrade. The response to RVI.NEMA-2.3 may satisfy this requirement.

Required Test Procedures

RTP.NEMA-7.1   Tester shall configure the Smart Meter as documented in the Vendor's response to RVI.NEMA-7.1, perform a successful Firmware Upgrade as documented in RTP.NEMA-3.1, and verify that the Smart Meter configuration persists via the methods in the Vendor's response to RVI.NEMA-7.2.

Test Steps

1. Tester shall install Image A on a Test Smart Meter.

2. Tester shall configure the Smart Meter as documented in the Vendor's response to RVI.NEMA-7.1.

3. Tester shall document the configuration.

4. Tester shall follow the methods in the Vendor's response to RVI.NEMA-3.1 to install Image B on the Test Smart Meter.

5. Based on the Vendor's response to RVI.NEMA-7.2, Tester shall verify that the Smart Meter's configuration persisted by comparing to the configuration documented in test step 3.

Test Results and Records

1. Tester shall record all Required Vendor Information that was used for the test.

2. Tester shall record all messages, responses, and event log records created during the test.

3. The test passes if all Test Steps complete successfully and Tester was able to positively confirm step 4.

FR.NEMA-8   Metrology Continuation

Reference: NEMA SG-AMI 1-2009, Section 3.2.8

"Smart Meter shall continue the measurement and storage of Metered Data while receiving Firmware Image updates."

Conditionality: This Functional Requirement is mandatory for Smart Meters.

Required Vendor Information

RVI.NEMA-8.1 Vendor shall supply Tester with two firmware images, Image A to be present on the Smart Meter before the upgrade, and Image B to be installed during the upgrade. The response to RVI.NEMA-2.3 may satisfy this requirement.

Required Test Procedures

RTP.NEMA-8.1 Tester shall place the meter under a known load and monitor load profile data during a successful firmware upgrade process as documented in RTP.NEMA-3.1 and verify that measurement and storage of Metered Data is not interrupted by the update process.

Test Steps

1. Tester shall install Image A on a Test Smart Meter.
2. Tester shall configure the test environment so that the Test Smart Meter is metering electricity at a measurable rate.
3. Tester shall follow the methods in the Vendor's response to RVI.NEMA-3.1 to install Image B on the Test Smart Meter.
4. Tester shall confirm that the measurement and storage of Metered Data is not interrupted.

Test Results and Records

1. Tester shall record all Required Vendor Information that was used for the test.
2. Tester shall record all messages, responses, and event log records created during the test.
3. The test passes if all Test Steps complete successfully and Tester was able to positively confirm step 4.

FR.NEMA-9   Initiation of Firmware Upgrade Activation

Reference: NEMA SG-AMI 1-2009, Section 3.2.9

"Smart Meter shall support a mechanism for coordinating activation of Firmware Image updates. Specifically, the Smart Meter shall not activate the new Firmware Image until instructed to do so."

Conditionality: This Functional Requirement is mandatory for Smart Meters.

Required Vendor Information

RVI.NEMA-9.1 Vendor shall document the method for uploading a Firmware Image, clearly indicating how the Smart Meter is instructed to activate the Firmware as a separate step from uploading.

RVI.NEMA-9.2 Vendor shall document the method for activating a Firmware Upgrade.

RVI.NEMA-9.3 Vendor shall supply Tester with two firmware images, Image A to be present on the Smart Meter before the upgrade, and Image B to be installed during the upgrade. The response to RVI.NEMA-2.3 may satisfy this requirement.

Required Test Procedures

RTP.NEMA-9.1   Tester shall verify that the Activation function is distinct from the firmware upload to the Smart Meter.

Test Steps

1. Tester shall review the Vendor's response to RVI.NEMA-9.1 and RVI.NEMA-9.2 and confirm that the method for uploading a Firmware Image is different from the method for activating a Firmware Upgrade.

Test Results and Records

1. Tester shall record all Required Vendor Information that was used for the test.

2. The test passes if all Test Steps complete successfully and Tester was able to positively confirm step 1.

RTP.NEMA-9.2   Tester shall upload the firmware as documented in the Vendor's response to RVI.NEMA-9.1, and verify that the firmware upgrade does not take place.

Test Steps

1. Tester shall install Image A on a Test Smart Meter.

2. Tester shall follow the methods in the Vendor's response to RVI.NEMA-9.1 to upload Image B on the Test Smart Meter.

3. Tester shall invoke the firmware version identification method as documented by the Vendor in response to RVI.NEMA-1.2, and record the version returned.

4. Tester shall confirm that the version returned matches the version for Image A.

Test Results and Records

1. Tester shall record all Required Vendor Information that was used for the test.

2. Tester shall record all messages, responses, and event log records created during the test.

3. The test passes if all Test Steps complete successfully and Tester was able to positively confirm step 4.

RTP.NEMA-9.3   Tester shall activate the firmware upgrade as documented in the Vendor's response to RVI.NEMA-9.2 and verify that the firmware upgrade does take place without the activation function as documented in the Vendor's response to RVI.NEMA-9.1.

Test Steps

1. Tester shall install Image A on a Test Smart Meter.

2. Tester shall follow the methods in the Vendor's response to RVI.NEMA-9.1 to upload Image B on the Test Smart Meter.

3. Tester shall follow the methods in the Vendor's response to RVI.NEMA-9.2 to activate the installation of Image B on the Test Smart Meter.

4. Tester shall invoke the firmware version identification method as documented by the Vendor in response to RVI.NEMA-1.2, and record the version returned.

5. Tester shall confirm that the version returned matches the version for Image B.

Test Results and Records

1. Tester shall record all Required Vendor Information that was used for the test.

2. Tester shall record all messages, responses, and event log records created during the test.

3. The test passes if all Test Steps complete successfully and Tester was able to positively confirm step 5.

FR.NEMA-10 Firmware Upgrade Authorization

Reference: NEMA SG-AMI 1-2009, Section 3.2.10

"Smart Meter Upgrade Process shall require authorized initiation."

Conditionality: This Functional Requirement is mandatory for Smart Meters.

Required Vendor Information

RVI.NEMA-10.1   Vendor shall document how Firmware Upgrade Authorization is enforced. Documentation shall explain how the authorization process works, including the authentication method and the means to ensure that the authenticated user has authorization to upgrade the firmware.

RVI.NEMA-10.2   Vendor shall supply Tester with two firmware images, Image A to be present on the Smart Meter before the upgrade, and Image B to be installed during the upgrade. The response to RVI.NEMA-2.3 may satisfy this requirement.

Required Test Procedures

RTP.NEMA-10.1   Tester shall verify that the Firmware Upgrade process requires a command from an authorized user and it completes successfully when an authorized user initiates it.

Test Steps

1. Tester shall install Image A on a Test Smart Meter.

2. Using the credentials of an authorized user as documented in the Vendor's response to RVI.NEMA-10.1, Tester shall follow the methods in the Vendor's response to RVI.NEMA-3.1 to install Image B on the Test Smart Meter.

3. Tester shall invoke the firmware version identification function documented in the Vendor's response to RVI.NEMA-1.2 and record the version returned by the Test Smart Meter.

4. Tester shall confirm that the version returned matches the version for Image B.

Test Results and Records

1. Tester shall record all Required Vendor Information that was used for the test.

2. Tester shall record all messages, responses, and event log records created during the test.

3. The test passes if all Test Steps complete successfully and Tester was able to positively confirm step 4.

RTP.NEMA-10.2   Tester shall verify that the Firmware Upgrade process fails if initiated by an unauthorized user.

Test Steps

1. Tester shall install Image A on a Test Smart Meter.

2. Using the credentials of an unauthorized user as documented in the Vendor's response to RVI.NEMA-10.1, Tester shall follow the methods in the Vendor's response to RVI.NEMA-3.1 to attempt to install Image B on the Test Smart Meter.

3. Tester shall invoke the firmware version identification function documented in the Vendor's response to RVI.NEMA-1.2 and record the version returned by the Test Smart Meter.

4. Tester shall confirm that the version returned matches the version for Image A.

Test Results and Records

1. Tester shall record all Required Vendor Information that was used for the test.

2. Tester shall record all messages, responses, and event log records created during the test.

3. The test passes if all Test Steps complete successfully and Tester was able to positively confirm step 4.

RTP.NEMA-10.3   Tester shall verify that the Firmware Upgrade process fails if initiated without authentication.

Test Steps

1. Tester shall install Image A on a Test Smart Meter.

2. If possible, Tester shall follow the methods in the Vendor's response to RVI.NEMA-3.1 to install Image B on the Test Smart Meter without authenticating as documented in the Vendor's response to RVI.NEMA-10.1.

3. Tester shall invoke the firmware version identification function documented in the Vendor's response to RVI.NEMA-1.2 and record the version returned by the Test Smart Meter.

4. Tester shall confirm that the version returned matches the version for Image B.

Test Results and Records

1. Tester shall record all Required Vendor Information that was used for the test.

2. Tester shall record all messages, responses, and event log records created during the test.

3. The test passes if all Test Steps complete successfully and Tester was able to positively confirm step 4.

FR.NEMA-11 Firmware Authentication

Reference: NEMA SG-AMI 1-2009, Section 3.2.11

"Smart Meter shall validate that the Firmware Image comes from a trusted source."

Conditionality: This Functional Requirement is mandatory for Smart Meters.

Required Vendor Information

RVI.NEMA-11.1   Vendor shall document how the Smart Meter validates that the Firmware Image comes from a trusted source.

RVI.NEMA-11.2   Vendor shall supply Tester with two firmware images, Image A to be present on the Smart Meter before the upgrade, and the untrusted Image D. If digital certificates are used to validate the Firmware Image, "untrusted" means based on certificates that were not issued by trusted keys, expired certificates, and revoked certificates. In this case, Images D1, D2, and D3 shall be produced according to those three scenarios. If another mechanism is used, an Image D shall be produced exhibiting each failure mode in the trust process.

Required Test Procedures

RTP.NEMA-11.1   Tester shall examine Image A to verify that data authentication information is present and formatted as described in the Vendor's response to RVI.NEMA-11.1.

Test Steps

1. Tester shall examine Image A and verify that data authentication information is present and formatted as described in the Vendor's response to RVI.NEMA-11.1.

This is the positive test case for the firmware authentication check process. This test is satisfied by completion of RTP.NEMA-3.1.

Test Results and Records

1. Tester shall record all Required Vendor Information that was used for the test.

2. The test passes if Tester was able to positively confirm step 1.

RTP.NEMA-11.2   Tester shall perform the Firmware Upgrade process with each of the D images provided by the vendor in response to RVI.NEMA-11.2 and verify that the process fails.

Test Steps

1. Tester shall install Image A on a Test Smart Meter.

2. Tester shall follow the methods in the Vendor's response to RVI.NEMA-3.1 to install Image D1 on the Test Smart Meter.

3. Tester shall invoke the firmware version identification function documented in the Vendor's response to RVI.NEMA-1.2 and record the version returned by the Test Smart Meter.

4. Tester shall record how the Smart Meter fails in response to the failure to trust the source of the firmware.

5. Tester shall confirm that the version returned matches the version for Image A.

6. Tester shall repeat these steps for each Image D.

Test Results and Records

1. Tester shall record all Required Vendor Information that was used for the test.

2. Tester shall record all messages, responses, and event log records created during the test.

3. The test passes if all Test Steps complete successfully and Tester was able to positively confirm step 4.

FR.NEMA-12 Cryptographic Algorithms

Reference: NEMA SG-AMI 1-2009, Section 4.1

"Cryptographic algorithms shall be current, publicly vetted, and government-approved."

Conditionality: This Functional Requirement is mandatory for Smart Meters.

Required Vendor Information

RVI.NEMA-12.1   Vendor shall list all cryptographic algorithms supported by the Smart Meter under test. If the Smart Meter uses a cryptographic module validated for conformance to FIPS 140-2[8] [FIPS 140] or later, the cryptographic module's Security Policy will suffice to meet this requirement. If the Smart Meter uses cryptographic algorithms that have been validated by the Cryptographic Algorithm Validation Program or by other recognized authority, vendor shall provide proof of validation.

Required Test Procedures

RTP.NEMA-12.1   Tester shall determine whether the cryptographic algorithms used are current, publicly vetted, and government-approved.

Test Steps

1. Tester shall confirm that all cryptographic algorithms identified in the Vendor's response to RVI.NEMA-12.1 are government-approved. In the United States, government-approved algorithms are those included in NIST's Cryptographic Algorithm Validation Program (CAVP). [9] Note that validation of the

---

[8] http://csrc.nist.gov/groups/STM/cmvp/index.html
[9] http://csrc.nist.gov/groups/STM/cavp/index.html

algorithm implementations or cryptographic modules is not required by the standard.

Test Results and Records

1. Tester shall record all Required Vendor Information that was used for the test.

2. The test passes if all Test Steps complete successfully and Tester was able to positively confirm step 1.

FR.NEMA-13 Cryptography Strengths

Reference: NEMA SG-AMI 1-2009, Section 4.2

"Cryptography strengths shall support Smart Meters deployed toward the end of a product's life cycle and be designed to provide a useful twenty-year service life—at a minimum, those cryptography strength time spans noted in NIST Special Publication SP 800-57, Part 1 (revised March 2007)."

Conditionality: This Functional Requirement is mandatory for Smart Meters.

Required Vendor Information

RVI.NEMA-13.1   Vendor shall list all the key sizes used by the cryptographic algorithms.

Required Test Procedures

RTP.NEMA-13.1   Tester shall determine if the strengths identified by the vendor comply with a twenty-year duration cryptography strength time spans according the document cited in the requirement.

Test Steps

1. NIST Special Publication SP 800-57 Part 1 [SP800-57] Table 3 identifies 128 bits of key strength as necessary for a twenty-year security life for keys generated 2011 or later.

2. Tester shall refer to NIST Special Publication SP 800-57 Part 1 Table 2 to confirm that all key sizes identified in the Vendor's response to RVI.NEMA-13.1 provide 128 or more bits of security.

Test Results and Records

1. Tester shall record all Required Vendor Information that was used for the test.

2. The test passes if all Test Steps complete successfully and Tester was able to positively confirm step 2.

FR.NEMA-14 Resilient AMI System Design

Reference: NEMA SG-AMI 1-2009, Section 4.3

"AMI system design shall ensure that compromise of a single Smart Meter does not lead to compromise of the AMI system at large."

Conditionality: This Functional Requirement is mandatory for Smart Meters.

Required Vendor Information

RVI.NEMA-14.1   Vendor shall document the mechanisms that ensure that the Smart Meters in an AMI system do not use the same passwords and keys when operational. This could be accomplished by generating unique initial passwords and keys for all Smart Meters, or by requiring a change of passwords and keys during system configuration. If the Smart Meter enforces such a change of passwords and keys before operating, vendor documentation shall explain that process.

Required Test Procedures

RTP.NEMA-14.1   Tester shall verify that a Smart Meter that has been configured according to Vendor guidance does not share default passwords or keys.

Test Steps

1. Tester shall follow the procedures documented in RVI.NEMA-14.1 to install and configure a Test Smart Meter.

2. Tester shall verify that all passwords and keys used by the Test Smart Meter have been randomly generated or generated by the Tester during the installation and configuration process.

Test Results and Records

1. Tester shall record all Required Vendor Information that was used for the test.

2. The test passes if all Test Steps complete successfully and Tester was able to positively confirm step 2.

FR.NEMA-15 Authentication and Integrity of Command Messages

Reference: NEMA SG-AMI 1-2009, Section 4.4

"Security protections shall provide strong authentication and integrity mechanisms to ensure that command messages to and from Smart Meters are not altered in transit or forged."

Conditionality: This Functional Requirement is mandatory for Smart Meters.

Required Vendor Information

RVI.NEMA-15.1   Vendor shall document what security protections the Smart Meter provides for command messages.

Required Test Procedures

RTP.NEMA-15.1   If the Smart Meter provides security protections for command messages, Tester shall confirm that the authentication and integrity mechanisms are in place.

Test Steps

1. Tester shall attempt to issue commands to the Smart Meter using incorrect authentication credentials, and verify that the commands fail and the authentication errors are logged.

2. Tester shall attempt to issue commands with the integrity mechanism subverted, and verify that the commands fail and the integrity errors are logged.

Test Results and Records

1. Tester shall record all Required Vendor Information that was used for the test.

2. The test passes if all Test Steps complete successfully and Tester was able to positively confirm steps 1 and 2.

RTP.NEMA-15.2   If the Smart Meter relies on another component to provide security protections for command messages, clearly indicate this in the Test Report.

FR.NEMA-16 Security Protections on Firmware Upgrade and Disconnect

Reference: NEMA SG-AMI 1-2009, Section 4.5

"Security protections shall extend to all field operation commands within the Smart Meter, with particular attention to operating the disconnect switch and modifying the device Firmware Image."

Conditionality: This Functional Requirement is mandatory for Smart Meters.

Required Vendor Information

RVI.NEMA-16.1   Vendor shall document all security protections on field operation commands within the Smart Meter.

Required Test Procedures

RTP.NEMA-16.1   If the Smart Meter provides security protections on field operation commands, Tester shall confirm that security protections apply to remote disconnect and firmware upgrade functions.

Test Steps

1. Tester shall follow the vendor's instructions to initiate a firmware upgrade.

2. Tester shall verify that the security protections identified in RVI.NEMA-16.1 are required to perform the firmware upgrade.

3. If the Test Smart Meter supports a remote disconnect capability, Tester shall follow the vendor's instructions to initiate the remote disconnect.

4. Tester shall verify that the security protections identified in RVI.NEMA-16.1 are required to perform the remote disconnect.

Test Results and Records

1. Tester shall record all Required Vendor Information that was used for the test.

2. The test passes if all Test Steps complete successfully and Tester was able to positively confirm steps 2 and 4.

RTP.NEMA-16.2   If the Smart Meter relies on another component to provide security protections on field operation commands, Tester shall clearly indicate this in the Test Report.

FR.NEMA-18 Forgery Protection

Reference: NEMA SG-AMI 1-2009, Section 4.7

"Security protections shall provide protection against forgery of Smart Meter data."

Conditionality: This Functional Requirement is mandatory for Smart Meters.

Required Vendor Information

RVI.NEMA-18.1   Vendor shall document all security protections provided by the Smart Meter that protect against forgery of Smart Meter data.

Required Test Procedures

RTP.NEMA-18.1   If Smart Meter provides security protections against forgery of Smart Meter data, Tester shall confirm that security protections identified in the Vendor's response to RVI.NEMA-18.1 work properly.

Test Steps

1. Tester shall verify that the security protections listed in RVI.NEMA-18.1 are in place.

Test Results and Records

1. Tester shall record all Required Vendor Information that was used for the test.

2. The test passes if all Test Steps complete successfully and Tester was able to positively confirm step 1.

RTP.NEMA-18.2   If the Smart Meter relies on another component to provide security protections against forgery of Smart Meter data, Tester shall clearly indicate this in the Test Report.

FR.NEMA-19 Defense-in-Depth from HAN

Reference: NEMA SG-AMI 1-2009, Section 4.8

"AMI systems shall employ a defense-in-depth strategy that shields Smart Grid Communication Networks from Home Area Networks."

Conditionality: It is mandatory for Smart Meters to support this AMI system design requirement.

Required Vendor Information

RVI.NEMA-19.1   Vendor shall document all measures the Smart Meter takes to shield the Smart Grid Communication Networks from Home Area Networks.

Required Test Procedures

RTP.NEMA-19.1   Tester shall confirm that security protections identified in the Vendor's response to RVI.NEMA-19.1 work properly.

Test Steps

1. Tester shall verify that the security protections listed in RVI.NEMA-19.1 are in place.

Test Results and Records

1. Tester shall record all Required Vendor Information that was used for the test.

2. The test passes if all Test Steps complete successfully and Tester was able to positively confirm step 1.

FR.NEMA-20 Intrusion Detection

Reference: NEMA SG-AMI 1-2009, Section 4.9

"AMI systems shall support anomaly and/or intrusion detection that indicate that Smart Meters may have been compromised, or when abnormal activity is detected."

Conditionality: It is mandatory for Smart Meters to support this AMI system design requirement.

Required Vendor Information

RVI.NEMA-20.1   Vendor shall document how the Smart Meter supports a systematic anomaly and/or intrusion detection capability, including what conditions are detected and what alarms or messages are generated in response.

Required Test Procedures

RTP.NEMA-20.1   Tester shall verify that the functions the Smart Meter implements in support of a systematic intrusion detection capability work as documented in the Vendor's response to RVI.NEMA-20.1.

Test Steps

1. Tester shall attempt to trigger the intrusion detection mechanism, and verify that the expected alarms or messages are generated in response.

Test Results and Records

1. Tester shall record all Required Vendor Information that was used for the test.

2. The test passes if all Test Steps complete successfully and Tester was able to positively confirm step 1.

FR.NEMA-21 Log Authentication and Encryption Failures

Reference: NEMA SG-AMI 1-2009, Section 4.10

"Logging and auditing mechanism shall be in place to show when authentication or encrypted communications fail."

Conditionality: This Functional Requirement is mandatory for Smart Meters.

Required Vendor Information

RVI.NEMA-21.1   Vendor shall document the technique by which authentication failures are logged.

RVI.NEMA-21.2   Vendor shall document the technique by which encrypted communications failures are logged.

Required Test Procedures

RTP.NEMA-21.1	RVI.NEMA-15.1 step 1 verifies that authentication failures are logged.
RTP.NEMA-21.2	Tester shall verify the technique by which encrypted communications failures are logged, and test the correct implementation of the auditing mechanism and that the data logged is accurate and complete.

Test Steps

1. Test step 1 of RTP.NEMA-15.1 verifies that authentication failures are logged.

2. Tester shall induce a failure of encrypted communications and verify that the failure is logged.

Test Results and Records

1. Tester shall record all Required Vendor Information that was used for the test.

2. The test passes if all Test Steps complete successfully and Tester was able to positively confirm step 1 and 2.

3. Conformance Tests for Conditional Requirements Applicable to Smart Meters

The following functional requirements are mandatory if certain conditions are met. They are excluded from the mandatory Conformance Test Requirements either because they require security protections that can be provided either by the Smart Meter itself or by the AMI Network, or because the Smart Meter can choose from multiple ways to meet a mandatory requirement. If a Smart Meter vendor implements these requirements within the Smart Meter, then to demonstrate conformance to these requirements, they shall use the methods below.

FR.NEMA-2a Firmware Upgrade Recovery to Previously Installed Firmware

Reference: NEMA SG-AMI 1-2009, Section 3.2.2

"Smart Meter shall recover to the previously installed Firmware ... if unable to complete the Upgrade Process."

Conditionality: This Functional Requirement is mandatory for Smart Meters that recover to previously installed Firmware according to the Vendor's response to RVI-NEMA-2.1.

Required Vendor Information

RVI.NEMA-2a.1   Vendor shall document the process by which the Smart Meter recovers to the previously installed Firmware.

RVI.NEMA-2a.2   Vendor shall supply Tester with two firmware images, Image A to be present on the Smart Meter before the upgrade, and Image B to be installed during the upgrade. The response to RVI.NEMA-2.3 may satisfy this requirement.

Required Test Procedures

RTP.NEMA-2a.1   Tester shall induce a failure in the firmware upgrade process and verify that the Smart Meter recovers to the previously installed firmware (using the firmware version identification function documented in the Vendor's response to RVI.NEMA-1.1).

Test Steps

1. Tester shall install Image A on a Test Smart Meter.

2. Tester shall follow the methods in the Vendor's response to RVI.NEMA-3.1 to initiate the installation of Image B on the Test Smart Meter.

3. Tester shall induce a failure in the installation process.

4. Tester shall invoke the firmware version identification function documented in the Vendor's response to RVI.NEMA-1.2 and record the version returned by the Test Smart Meter.

5. Tester shall confirm that the version returned matches the version for Image A.

Test Results and Records

1. Tester shall record all Required Vendor Information that was used for the test.

2. Tester shall record all messages, responses, and event log records created during the test.

3. The test passes if all Test Steps complete successfully and Tester was able to positively confirm step 5.

FR.NEMA-2b Firmware Upgrade Recovery Failed Upgrade Process Alarm

Reference: NEMA SG-AMI 1-2009, Section 3.2.2

"Smart Meter shall ... initiate a "Failed Upgrade Process" alarm to the Network Management System or the Upgrade Management System if unable to complete the Upgrade Process."

Conditionality: This Functional Requirement is mandatory for Smart Meters that initiate a "Failed Upgrade Process" alarm according to the Vendor's response to RVI-NEMA-2.1.

Required Vendor Information

RVI.NEMA-2b.1   Vendor shall document how to identify the Failed Upgrade Process alarm (i.e., where the alarm is sent, the alarm properties, etc.).

RVI.NEMA-2b.2   Vendor shall supply Tester with two firmware images, Image A to be present on the Smart Meter before the upgrade, and Image B to be installed during the upgrade. The response to RVI.NEMA-2.3 may satisfy this requirement.

Required Test Procedures

RTP.NEMA-2b.1   Tester shall induce a failure in the upgrade process and verify that the Smart Meter sends an alarm as described in the Vendor's response to RVI.NEMA-2b.1.

Test Steps

1. Tester shall install Image A on a Test Smart Meter.

2. Tester shall follow the methods in the Vendor's response to RVI.NEMA-3.1 to initiate the installation of Image B on the Test Smart Meter.

3. Tester shall induce a failure in the installation process.

4. Tester shall confirm that a Failed Upgrade Process alarm is sent as specified in the vendor response to RVI.NEMA-2b.1.

Test Results and Records

1. Tester shall record all Required Vendor Information that was used for the test.

2. Tester shall record all messages, responses, and event log records created during the test.

3. The test passes if all Test Steps complete successfully and Tester was able to positively confirm step 4.

4. Conformance Tests for Optional Requirements Applicable to Smart Meters

The following Functional Requirements are optional, and the vendor may choose to implement solutions that satisfy them or may elect their own alternative. If a vendor implements within the Smart Meter solutions that satisfy these requirements, then the methods below may be used to demonstrate conformance to these requirements.

FR.NEMA-2c Firmware Upgrade Recovery Safe Inactive Mode

Reference: NEMA SG-AMI 1-2009, Section 3.2.2

"… if the Smart Meter has detected a hardware failure during the Upgrade Process (such as failed Electrically-Erasable Read Only Memory, or EEROM), the Smart Meter may alternatively enter into a safe inactive mode."

Conditionality: This Functional Requirement is optional for Smart Meters. Smart Meters that support an inactive mode upon hardware failure may incorporate this Functional Requirement.

Required Vendor Information

RVI.NEMA-2c.1   Vendor shall document how the Smart Meter enters and recovers from the safe inactive mode.

RVI.NEMA-2c.2   Vendor shall supply Tester with two firmware images, Image A to be present on the Smart Meter before the upgrade, and Image B to be installed during the upgrade. The response to RVI.NEMA-2.3 may satisfy this requirement.

Required Test Procedures

RTP.NEMA-2c.1   Tester shall induce a hardware failure in the firmware upgrade process and verify that the Smart Meter enters an inactive mode.

Test Steps

1. Tester shall install Image A on a Test Smart Meter.

2. Tester shall follow the methods in the Vendor's response to RVI.NEMA-3.1 to initiate the installation of Image B on the Test Smart Meter.

3. Tester shall induce a failure in the installation process.

4. Tester shall verify that the meter enters the safe inactive mode as documented in the vendor response to RVI.NEMA-2c.1.

Test Results and Records

1. Tester shall record all Required Vendor Information that was used for the test.

2. Tester shall record all messages, responses, and event log records created during the test.

3. The test passes if all Test Steps complete successfully and Tester was able to positively confirm step 4.

5. Non-testable Requirements for Smart Meters

This section lists the Functional Requirements deemed not to be written in a testable manner.

FR.NEMA-17 Operational and Privacy Requirements Support

Reference: NEMA SG-AMI 1-2009, Section 4.6

"Security protections shall support both the operational needs of utilities and the privacy needs of customers. This does not exclude, replace, or eliminate the need for security protections outside the Smart Meter."

Conditionality: N/A, not a testable requirement.

Required Vendor Information

N/A

Required Test Procedures

N/A

6. Conformance Tests for Mandatory Requirements for Upgrade Management Systems

The following Functional Requirements are mandatory for Upgrade Management Systems. It is important to note that Functional Requirement FR.NEMA-24 for Upgrade Management System invokes the same security Functional Requirements (FR.NEMA-12 through FR.NEMA-21) as for the Smart Meters.

FR.NEMA-22 Upgrade Management System Initiation of Firmware Upgrade Activation

Reference: NEMA SG-AMI 1-2009, Section 3.6.1

"Upgrade Management System shall support a mechanism for coordinating activation of Firmware Image updates."

Conditionality: This Functional Requirement is mandatory for Upgrade Management Systems.

Required Vendor Information

RVI.NEMA-22.1   Vendor shall document the method for uploading a Firmware Image.

RVI.NEMA-22.2   Vendor shall document the method for activating a Firmware Upgrade.

RVI.NEMA-22.3   Vendor shall supply Tester with two firmware images, Image A to be present on the Smart Meter before the upgrade, and Image B to be installed during the upgrade. The response to RVI.NEMA-2.3 may satisfy this requirement.

Required Test Procedures

RTP.NEMA-22.1   Tester shall verify that the Activation function is distinct from the firmware upload to the Smart Meter.

Test Steps

1. Tester shall review the Vendor's response to RVI.NEMA-22.1 and RVI.NEMA-22.2 and confirm that the method for uploading a Firmware Image is different from the method for activating a Firmware Upgrade.

Test Results and Records

1. Tester shall record all Required Vendor Information that was used for the test.

2. The test passes if all Test Steps complete successfully and Tester was able to positively confirm step 1.

RTP.NEMA-22.2   Tester shall upload the firmware as documented in the Vendor's response to RVI.NEMA-22.1 and verify that the firmware upgrade does not take place.

Test Steps

1. Tester shall install Image A on a Test Smart Meter.

2. Tester shall follow the methods in the Vendor's response to RVI.NEMA-22.1 to upload Image B on the Test Smart Meter.

3. Tester shall invoke the firmware version identification method as documented by the Vendor in response to RVI.NEMA-1.2 and record the version returned.

4. Tester shall confirm that the version returned matches the version for Image A.

Test Results and Records

1. Tester shall record all Required Vendor Information that was used for the test.

2. Tester shall record all messages, responses, and event log records created during the test.

3. The test passes if all Test Steps complete successfully and Tester was able to positively confirm step 4.

RTP.NEMA-22.3   Tester shall activate the firmware upgrade as documented in the Vendor's response to RVI.NEMA-22.2.

Test Steps

1. Tester shall install Image A on a Test Smart Meter.

2. Tester shall follow the methods in the Vendor's response to RVI.NEMA-22.1 to upload Image B on the Test Smart Meter.

3. Tester shall follow the methods in the Vendor's response to RVI.NEMA-22.2 to activate the installation of Image B on the Test Smart Meter.

4. Tester shall invoke the firmware version identification method as documented by the Vendor in response to RVI.NEMA-1.2 and record the version returned.

5. Tester shall confirm that the version returned matches the version for Image B.

Test Results and Records

1. Tester shall record all Required Vendor Information that was used for the test.

2. Tester shall record all messages, responses, and event log records created during the test.

3. The test passes if all Test Steps complete successfully and Tester was able to positively confirm step 5.

FR.NEMA-23 Upgrade Management System Firmware Upgrade Recovery to Previously Installed Firmware

Reference: NEMA SG-AMI 1-2009, Section 3.6.2

"Upgrade Management System shall support a process to restore previous installed Firmware Image if unable to complete the Upgrade Process."

Conditionality:	This Functional Requirement is mandatory for Upgrade Management Systems.

Required Vendor Information

RVI.NEMA-23.1	Vendor shall document the process by which the Upgrade Management System supports the process to restore previous installed Firmware if unable to complete the Upgrade Process.
RVI.NEMA-23.2	Vendor shall supply Tester with two firmware images, Image A to be present on the Smart Meter before the upgrade, and Image B to be installed during the upgrade. The response to RVI.NEMA-2.3 may satisfy this requirement.

Required Test Procedures

RTP.NEMA-23.1	Tester shall induce a failure in the firmware upgrade process and verify that the Upgrade Management System restores to the previously installed firmware (using the firmware version identification function documented in the Vendor's response to RVI.NEMA-1.1).

Test Steps

1. Tester shall install Image A on a Test Smart Meter.
2. Tester shall initiate the process to upgrade to Image B and induce a failure in the upgrade process.
3. Tester shall invoke the firmware version identification method as documented by the Vendor in response to RVI.NEMA-1.2 and record the version returned.
4. Tester shall confirm that the version returned matches the version for Image A.

Test Results and Records

1. Tester shall record all Required Vendor Information that was used for the test.
2. Tester shall record all messages, responses, and event log records created during the test.
3. The test passes if all Test Steps complete successfully and Tester was able to positively confirm step 4.

FR.NEMA-24 Upgrade Management System Upgrade Process Security Requirements

Reference: NEMA SG-AMI 1-2009, Section 3.6.3

"Upgrade Management System Upgrade Process shall follow the Section 4 Upgrade Process Security Requirements."

Conditionality:	This Functional Requirement is mandatory for Upgrade Management Systems.

Required Vendor Information

RVI.NEMA-24.1	Vendor shall meet all Required Vendor Information listed for Smart Meters in the Functional Requirements as indicated in Table 1 above with (Y).

Required Test Procedures

RTP.NEMA-24.1 Tester shall verify that the Upgrade Management System is also conformant to Functional Requirements as indicated in Table 1 above with (Y).

FR.NEMA-25 Log Firmware Upgrade Attempts and Results

Reference: NEMA SG-AMI 1-2009, Section 3.6.4

"Upgrade Management System shall log Upgrade Process attempts and results."

Conditionality: This Functional Requirement is mandatory for Upgrade Management Systems.

Required Vendor Information

RVI.NEMA-25.1 Vendor shall document how the Upgrade Management System logs Upgrade Process attempts and results.

RVI.NEMA-25.2 Vendor shall supply Tester with two firmware images, Image A to be present on the Smart Meter before the upgrade, and Image B to be installed during the upgrade. The response to RVI.NEMA-2.3 may satisfy this requirement.

Required Test Procedures

RTP.NEMA-25.1 Tester shall perform a successful firmware upgrade process and verify that the upgrade attempt and successful results are logged by the Upgrade Management System.

Test Steps

1. Tester shall install Image A on a Test Smart Meter.

2. Tester shall follow the procedures to upgrade to Image B.

3. Tester shall verify that the upgrade attempt and successful results are both logged as described in the Vendor's response to RVI.NEMA-25.1.

Test Results and Records

1. Tester shall record all Required Vendor Information that was used for the test.

2. Tester shall record all messages, responses, and event log records created during the test.

3. The test passes if all Test Steps complete successfully and Tester was able to positively confirm step 3.

RTP.NEMA-25.2 Tester shall initiate a failed firmware upgrade process and verify that the upgrade attempt and unsuccessful results are logged by the Upgrade Management System.

Test Steps

1. Tester shall install Image A on a Test Smart Meter.

2. Tester shall initiate the process to upgrade to Image B and induce a failure in the upgrade process.

3. Tester shall verify that the upgrade attempt and unsuccessful results are both logged as described in the Vendor's response to RVI.NEMA-25.1.

Test Results and Records

1. Tester shall record all Required Vendor Information that was used for the test.

2. Tester shall record all messages, responses, and event log records created during the test.

3. The test passes if all Test Steps complete successfully and Tester was able to positively confirm step 3.

Annex A – Functional Requirements for Upgrade Management System and Smart Meter Tested together as a System-Under-Test

A.1 Introduction

At the time this test framework document is written, there is no standardized communication protocol between the Upgrade Management Systems (UMS) and Smart Meters, and testing these two components independently is not possible without developing customized conformance tests for each Smart Meter or UMS submitted for testing. Therefore, this Annex presents a test scenario in which the UMS and Smart Meter are provisioned together and are tested for conformance as a single System-Under-Test (SUT).

Because the Smart Meter and UMS are bundled, some tests for conformance to the Standard are not "conclusive"; i.e., if a specific test passes, it is not possible to conclude, with certainty, whether the test passes for the Smart Meter, UMS, or both devices. The tests for UMS Functional Requirements FR.NEMA-23, FR.NEMA-25, and FR.NEMA-22 are similar to the Smart Meter Functional Requirements FR.NEMA-2, FR.NEM-5, and FR.NEMA-9, respectively. However, these individual tests are "not conclusive" since the Smart Meter and UMS are tested together as a single System-Under-Test, and even when the conformance tests for these Functional Requirements pass, it is not possible to conclusively determine if each component satisfies its Functional Requirements.

For example, it is not possible, with certainty, to determine if the Smart Meter recovers to the previously installed image as required in FR.NEMA-2 or the UMS does so as required in FR.NEMA-23. Moreover, the conformance testing to the security requirements FR.NEMA-12 through FR.NEMA-21 listed in the Standard explicitly for Smart Meters and for Upgrade Management System implicitly through FR.NEMA-24, are also inconclusive, since it is impossible in this scenario to conclude without any doubt when a test completes successfully, if the Smart Meter or the UMS completed it. The Tester can only conclude that the System-Under-Test, which is the bundled of the two components, passed or failed the test.

Figure A.1 below shows an abstract model of a test setup for the UMS and Smart Meter to be tested as a bundle. The UMS and the Smart Meter together are referred to as the System-Under-Test. The test setup includes the following components:
- The Test Application - that hosts any custom applications used to execute the tests; and
- The System-Under-Test – that consists of the Smart Meter (including the Metrology and Communications Modules) and the Upgrade Management System, along with any back-end components required to communicate and manage the upgrade process.

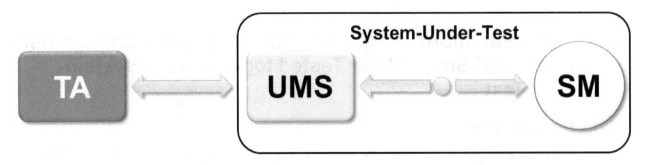

Figure A.1 - System Test Setup for Bundled UMS and SM

Table A.1 below lists the Functional Requirements that are applicable when testing an Upgrade Management System and Smart Meter bundled together as a System-Under-Test. The conditionality and applicability columns are as defined for Table 1 in Section 1.6.2. The conclusiveness column indicates whether the test steps for the Functional Requirement can be used to conclusively determine which component supports the requirement, as discussed above.

Table A.1 - Functional Requirements for SUT –
Conditionality, Applicability and Conclusiveness

Original Functional Requirement(s) / **SUT Functional Requirement(s)**	Conditionality	Applies to Smart Meter	Applies to UMS	SUT	Conclusiveness
FR.NEMA-1/	M	Y	N		
FR.NEMA-1 1A	M			Y	Y
FR.NEMA-2 &	M	Y	-		
FR.NEMA-23/	M	-	Y		
FR.NEMA-2A	M			Y	N
FR.NEMA-2a /	C	Y	N		
FR.NEMA-2Aa	C			Y	N
FR.NEMA-2b/	C	Y	N		
FR.NEMA-2Ab	C			Y	Y
FR.NEMA-2c /	O	Y	N		
FR.NEMA-2Ac	O			Y	Y
FR.NEMA-3 /	M	Y	N		
FR.NEMA-3A	M			Y	Y
FR.NEMA-4 /	M	Y	N		
FR.NEMA-4A	M			Y	Y
FR.NEMA-5 &	M	Y	-		
FR.NEMA-25/	M	-	Y		
FR.NEMA-5A	M			Y	N
FR.NEMA-6 /	M	Y	N		
FR.NEMA-6A	M			Y	Y
FR.NEMA-7 /	M	Y	N		
FR.NEMA-7A	M			Y	Y
FR.NEMA-8 /	M	Y	N		
FR.NEMA-8A	M			Y	Y
FR.NEMA-9 &	M	Y	-		
FR.NEMA-22/	M	-	Y		

FR.NEMA-9A	M				Y	N
FR.NEMA.10 /	M	Y	N			
FR.NEMA-10A	M				Y	Y
FR.NEMA-11 /	M	Y	N			
FR.NEMA-11A	M				Y	Y
FR.NEMA-12 &	M	Y	-			
FR.NEMA-24 /	M	-	Y			
FR.NEMA-12A	M				Y	N
FR.NEMA-13 &	M	Y	-			
FR.NEMA-24/	M	-	Y			
FR.NEMA-13A	M				Y	N
FR.NEMA-14&	M	Y	-			
FR.NEMA-24 /	M	-	Y			
FR.NEMA-14A	M				Y	N
FR.NEMA-15 &	M	Y	-			
FR.NEMA-24/	M	-	Y			
FR.NEMA-15A	M				Y	N
FR.NEMA-16 &	M	Y	-			N
FR.NEMA-24/	M	-	Y			
FR.NEMA-16A	M				Y	
FR.NEMA-17 &	N	N	-			
FR.NEMA-24/	N	-	N			
FR.NEMA-17A	N				N	N/A
FR.NEMA-18 &	M	Y	-			
FR.NEMA-24/	M	-	Y			
FR.NEMA-18A	M				Y	N
FR.NEMA-19 &	M	Y	-			
FR.NEMA-24 /	M	-	Y			
FR.NEMA-19A	M				Y	N
FR.NEMA-20 &	M	Y	-			
FR.NEMA-24/	M	-	Y			
FR.NEMA-20A	M				Y	N
FR.NEMA-21 &	M	Y	-			
FR.NEMA-24/	M	-	Y			
FR.NEMA-21A	M				Y	N

A.2   Conformance Tests for Mandatory Requirements for SUT

The mandatory Functional Requirements and associated Required Vendor Information and Required Test Procedures for Upgrade Management Systems and Smart Meters tested together as a System-Under-Test are listed below.

FR.NEMA-1A Firmware Version Identification

Reference: NEMA SG-AMI 1-2009, Section 3.2.1

"Smart Meter shall attest the current version identification of Firmware for each of its components as defined in 2.17 upon a query from the Network Management System or the Upgrade Management System."

Conditionality: This Functional Requirement is mandatory for an Upgrade Management System and Smart Meter tested together as a System-Under-Test.

41

Required Vendor Information

RVI.NEMA-1A.1   Vendor shall supply Tester with Image A and its version.

RVI.NEMA-1A.2   Vendor shall document the operations of the firmware version identification method.

Required Test Procedures

RTP.NEMA-1A.1   Tester shall verify that the firmware version identification security function implemented in the firmware image works as documented.

Test Steps

1. Tester shall install Image A supplied by the Vendor in response to RVI.NEMA-1A.1 on a Test Smart Meter.

2. Tester shall invoke the firmware version identification method as documented by the Vendor in response to RVI.NEMA-1A.2 and record the version returned.

3. Tester shall confirm the firmware version identification security function worked as documented.

4. Tester shall confirm that the version returned by the SUT matches the version claimed by the Vendor.

Test Results and Records

1. Tester shall record all Required Vendor Information that was used for the test.

2. Tester shall record all messages, responses, and event log records created during the test.

3. The test passes if all Test Steps complete successfully and Tester was able to positively confirm steps 3 and 4.

FR.NEMA-2A Firmware Upgrade Recovery

Reference: NEMA SG-AMI 1-2009, Section 3.2.2

"Smart Meter shall recover to the previously installed Firmware or initiate a "Failed Upgrade Process" alarm to the Network Management System or the Upgrade Management System if unable to complete the Upgrade Process."

Conditionality: This Functional Requirement is mandatory for an Upgrade Management System and Smart Meter tested together as a System-Under-Test.

Required Vendor Information

RVI.NEMA-2A.1   Vendor shall document whether the Smart Meter recovers to previously installed firmware or initiates a "Failed Upgrade Process" alarm. If the Smart Meter recovers to previously installed firmware, the Conditional Functional Requirement FR.NEMA-2Aa is required. If the Smart Meter initiates a "Failed Upgrade Process" alarm, the Conditional Functional Requirement FR.NEMA-2Ab is required.

RVI.NEMA-2A.2   Vendor shall document how the Smart Meter detects a failed Upgrade Process, and what actions are taken in response.

RVI.NEMA-2A.3	Vendor shall supply Tester with two firmware images, Image A to be present on the Smart Meter before the upgrade, and Image B to be installed during the upgrade.

Required Test Procedures

RTP.NEMA-2A.1	Based on the Vendor's response to RVI.NEMA-2A.1, the Tester shall verify that the SUT either recovers to previously installed firmware or initiates a "Failed Upgrade Process" alarm.

Test Steps

1. Tester shall review the Vendor's response to RVI.NEMA-2A.1 and determine how the SUT responds to being unable to complete the upgrade process.
2. Tester shall confirm that the responses include either a recovery to previously installed firmware or initiation of a "Failed Upgrade Process" alarm (or both).

Test Results and Records

1. Tester shall record all Required Vendor Information that was used for the test.
2. The test passes if all Test Steps complete successfully and Tester was able to positively confirm step 2.

RTP.NEMA-2A.2	Based on the Vendor's response to RVI.NEMA-2A.1, the Tester shall execute the Required Test Procedures for the Conditional Functional Requirement FR.NEMA-2Aa and/or FR.NEMA-2Ab.

FR.NEMA-3A Firmware Completeness Validation

Reference: NEMA SG-AMI 1-2009, Section 3.2.3

"Smart Meter shall validate that Firmware Image reception is complete before effecting upgrade."

Conditionality:	This Functional Requirement is mandatory for an Upgrade Management System and Smart Meter tested together as a System-Under-Test.

Required Vendor Information

RVI.NEMA-3A.1	End-user guidance documents shall detail how to perform a firmware upgrade.
RVI.NEMA-3A.2	Vendor shall document how the Smart Meter detects an incomplete firmware.
RVI.NEMA-3A.3	Vendor shall document the Smart Meter's response to an incomplete firmware.
RVI.NEMA-3A.4	Vendor shall supply Tester with two firmware images, Image A to be present on the Smart Meter before the upgrade, and Image B to be installed during the upgrade. The response to RVI.NEMA-2A.3 may satisfy this requirement.

Required Test Procedures

RTP.NEMA-3A.1   Tester shall conduct a successful firmware upgrade according to the methods in the Vendor's response to RVI.NEMA-3A.1. This is the positive test case for the firmware upgrade process.

Test Steps

1. Tester shall install Image A on a Test Smart Meter.

2. Tester shall follow the methods in the Vendor's response to RVI.NEMA-3A.1 to install Image B on the Test Smart Meter.

3. Tester shall invoke the firmware version identification function documented in the Vendor's response to RVI.NEMA-1A.2 and record the version returned by the SUT.

4. Tester shall confirm that the version returned matches the version for Image B.

Test Results and Records

1. Tester shall record all Required Vendor Information that was used for the test.

2. Tester shall record all messages, responses, and event log records created during the test.

3. The test passes if all Test Steps complete successfully and Tester was able to positively confirm step 4.

RTP.NEMA-3A.2   Tester shall initiate an incomplete firmware upgrade process by disrupting the reception of the Image B and verify that the upgrade does not take effect and that the responses documented in the Vendor's response to RVI.NEMA-3A.3 take place.

Test Steps

1. Tester shall install Image A on a Test Smart Meter.

2. Tester shall follow the methods in the Vendor's response to RVI.NEMA-3A.1 to initiate installation of Image B on the Test Smart Meter.

3. Tester shall interfere with delivery of the complete Image B, disrupting it.

4. Tester shall confirm that the SUT detects the incomplete image as described in the Vendor response to RVI.NEMA-3A.2.

5. Tester shall confirm that the SUT responds to the detection of the incomplete image as described in the Vendor response to RVI.NEMA-3A.3.

6. If Vendor's response to RVI.NEMA-3A.3 lists any of the operations identified in functional requirement FR.NEMA-2A, tester shall confirm that the Smart Meter passes FR.NEMA-2A.

Test Results and Records

1. Tester shall record all Required Vendor Information that was used for the test.

2. Tester shall record all messages, responses, and event log records created during the test.

3. The test passes if all Test Steps complete successfully and Tester was able to positively confirm steps 4 and 6.

FR.NEMA-4A Firmware Integrity Validation

Reference: NEMA SG-AMI 1-2009, Section 3.2.4

"Smart Meter shall validate that a Firmware Image passes Integrity Check before effecting upgrade."

Conditionality: This Functional Requirement is mandatory for an Upgrade Management System and Smart Meter tested together as a System-Under-Test.

Required Vendor Information

RVI.NEMA-4A.1 Vendor shall document how the Smart Meter performs integrity check on firmware.

RVI.NEMA-4A.2 Vendor shall document the Smart Meter's response to an integrity check failure.

RVI.NEMA-4A.3 Vendor shall provide any necessary tools to enable the Tester to send a firmware image with compromised integrity. If the UMS normally detects integrity errors and does not send the image, then an additional test tool may be required to test the mechanism implemented by the Smart Meter that validates the integrity check verification.

RVI.NEMA-4A.4 Vendor shall supply Tester with two firmware images, Image A to be present on the Smart Meter before the upgrade, and Image B to be installed during the upgrade. The response to RVI.NEMA-2A.3 may satisfy this requirement.

Required Test Procedures

RTP.NEMA-4A.1 This is the positive test case for the firmware upgrade integrity check process. This test is satisfied by completion of RTP.NEMA-3.1A. RTP.NEMA-4A.2 Tester shall initiate a firmware upgrade process with an integrity check firmware error and verify that the upgrade does not take effect and that the responses documented in the Vendor's response to RVI.NEMA-4A.2 take place.

Test Steps

1. Tester shall install Image A on a Test Smart Meter.

2. Based on the Vendor's response to RVI.NEMA-4A.1, Tester shall modify the fields that implement the integrity mechanism for Image B, creating the corrupted Image C.

3. Tester shall follow the methods in the Vendor's response to RVI.NEMA-3A.1 to attempt to install Image C on the Test Smart Meter.

4. Tester shall confirm that the SUT responds as documented in the Vendor's response to RVI.NEMA-4A.2.

5. If Vendor's response to RVI.NEMA-4A.2 lists any of the operations identified in functional requirement FR.NEMA-2A, tester shall confirm that the Smart Meter passes FR.NEMA-2A.

Test Results and Records

1. Tester shall record all Required Vendor Information that was used for the test.

2. Tester shall record all messages, responses, and event log records created during the test.

3. The test passes if all Test Steps complete successfully and Tester was able to positively confirm steps 4 and 6.

FR.NEMA-5A Log Firmware Upgrade Attempts and Results

Reference: NEMA SG-AMI 1-2009, Section 3.2.5

"Smart Meter Upgrade Process attempts and results shall be logged."

Conditionality: This Functional Requirement is mandatory for an Upgrade Management System and Smart Meter tested together as a System-Under-Test.

Required Vendor Information

RVI.NEMA-5A.1 Vendor shall document how the Smart Meter logs Firmware Upgrade attempts and results.

RVI.NEMA-5A.2 Vendor shall supply Tester with two firmware images, Image A to be present on the Smart Meter before the upgrade, and Image B to be installed during the upgrade. The response to RVI.NEMA-2A.3 may satisfy this requirement.

Required Test Procedures

RTP.NEMA-5A.1 Tester shall perform a successful firmware upgrade process and verify that the upgrade attempt and successful results are logged. This test may be satisfied by gathering the log information during a positive test case such as RTP.NEMA-3A.1.

Test Steps

1. Tester shall install Image A on a Test Smart Meter.

2. Tester shall follow the methods in the Vendor's response to RVI.NEMA-3A.1 to install Image B on the Test Smart Meter.

3. Based on the Vendor's response to RVI.NEMA-5A.1, Tester shall confirm that the Firmware Upgrade attempt was logged.

Test Results and Records

1. Tester shall record all Required Vendor Information that was used for the test.

2. Tester shall record all messages, responses, and event log records created during the test.

3. The test passes if all Test Steps complete successfully and Tester was able to positively confirm step 3.

RTP.NEMA-5A.2   For each negative test case involving an induced failure elsewhere in this document, Tester shall initiate a failed firmware upgrade process and verify that the upgrade attempt and unsuccessful results are logged.

Test Steps

1. Tester shall install Image A on a Test Smart Meter.

2. Tester shall follow the methods in the Vendor's response to RVI.NEMA-3A.1 to initiate installation of Image B on the Test Smart Meter.

3. Tester shall interfere with delivery of the complete Image B, disrupting it.

4. Based on the Vendor's response to RVI.NEMA-5A.1, Tester shall confirm that the Firmware Upgrade attempt was logged, with the failed results recorded.

5. Tester shall install Image A on a Test Smart Meter.

6. Based on the Vendor's response to RVI.NEMA-4A.1, Tester shall modify the fields that implement the integrity mechanism for Image B, creating the corrupted Image C.

7. Tester shall follow the methods in the Vendor's response to RVI.NEMA-3A.1 to attempt to install Image C on the Test Smart Meter.

8. Based on the Vendor's response to RVI.NEMA-5A.1, Tester shall confirm that the Firmware Upgrade attempt was logged, with the failed results recorded.

Test Results and Records

1. Tester shall record all Required Vendor Information that was used for the test.

2. Tester shall record all messages, responses, and event log records created during the test.

3. The test passes if all Test Steps complete successfully and Tester was able to positively confirm step 4 and 8.

FR.NEMA-6A No Metrology Recalibration

Reference: NEMA SG-AMI 1-2009, Section 3.2.6

"Smart Meter shall not require Metrology recalibration after Firmware upgrade."

Conditionality: This Functional Requirement is mandatory for an Upgrade Management System and Smart Meter tested together as a System-Under-Test.

Required Vendor Information

RVI.NEMA-6A.1   Vendor shall document how to determine whether a Smart Meter requires Metrology recalibration. One way of determining it is an accuracy test performed at various loads to confirm that readings remain within the specified meter class range. A WECO device is an example of calibration device that may be used.

RVI.NEMA-6A.2   Vendor shall supply Tester with two firmware images, Image A to be present on the Smart Meter before the upgrade, and Image B to be installed during the upgrade. The response to RVI.NEMA-2A.3 may satisfy this requirement.

Required Test Procedures

RTP.NEMA-6A.1   Tester shall perform a successful firmware upgrade process as documented in RTP.NEMA-3A.1 and follow the methods documented in the Vendor's response to RVI.NEMA-6A.1 to verify that the Smart Meter does not require Metrology recalibration.

Test Steps

1. Tester shall install Image A on a Test Smart Meter.

2. Tester shall follow the methods in the Vendor's response to RVI.NEMA-3A.1 to install Image B on the Test Smart Meter.

3. Based on the Vendor's response to RVI.NEMA-6A.1, Tester shall verify that the SUT does not require Metrology recalibration.

Test Results and Records

1. Tester shall record all Required Vendor Information that was used for the test.

2. Tester shall record all messages, responses, and event log records created during the test.

3. The test passes if all Test Steps complete successfully and Tester was able to positively confirm step 3.

FR.NEMA-7A Configuration Persistence

Reference: NEMA SG-AMI 1-2009, Section 3.2.7

"Smart Meter shall support persisting existing Configuration after Firmware upgrade."

Conditionality: This Functional Requirement is mandatory for an Upgrade Management System and Smart Meter tested together as a System-Under-Test.

Required Vendor Information

RVI.NEMA-7A.1   Vendor shall document how to configure a Smart Meter to persist the configuration after a firmware upgrade.

RVI.NEMA-7A.2   Vendor shall document how to review and when possible, export the configuration of a Smart Meter's configuration has changed.

RVI.NEMA-7A.3   Vendor shall supply Tester with two firmware images, Image A to be present on the Smart Meter before the upgrade, and Image B to be installed during the upgrade. The response to RVI.NEMA-2A.3 may satisfy this requirement.

Required Test Procedures

RTP.NEMA-7A.1   Tester shall configure the Smart Meter as documented in the Vendor's response to RVI.NEMA-7A.1, perform a successful Firmware Upgrade as documented in RTP.NEMA-3A.1, and verify that the Smart Meter configuration persists via the methods in the Vendor's response to RVI.NEMA-7A.2.

Test Steps

1. Tester shall install Image A on a Test Smart Meter.

2. Tester shall configure the Smart Meter as documented in the Vendor's response to RVI.NEMA-7A.1.

3. Tester shall document the Smart Meter's configuration

4. Tester shall follow the methods in the Vendor's response to RVI.NEMA-3A.1 to install Image B on the Test Smart Meter.

5. Based on the Vendor's response to RVI.NEMA-7A.2, Tester shall verify that the SUT's configuration persisted by comparing with the configuration documented in the test step 3 above.

Test Results and Records

1. Tester shall record all Required Vendor Information that was used for the test.

2. Tester shall record all messages, responses, and event log records created during the test.

3. The test passes if all Test Steps complete successfully and Tester was able to positively confirm step 4.

FR.NEMA-8A Metrology Continuation

Reference: NEMA SG-AMI 1-2009, Section 3.2.8

"Smart Meter shall continue the measurement and storage of Metered Data while receiving Firmware Image updates."

Conditionality: This Functional Requirement is mandatory for an Upgrade Management System and Smart Meter tested together as a System-Under-Test.

Required Vendor Information

RVI.NEMA-8A.1   Vendor shall supply Tester with two firmware images, Image A to be present on the Smart Meter before the upgrade, and Image B to be installed during the upgrade. The response to RVI.NEMA-2A.3 may satisfy this requirement.

Required Test Procedures

RTP.NEMA-8A.1   Tester shall place the meter under a known load and monitor load profile data during a successful firmware upgrade process as documented in RTP.NEMA-3A.1 and verify that measurement and storage of Metered Data is not interrupted by the update process.

Test Steps

1. Tester shall install Image A on a Test Smart Meter.

2. Tester shall configure the test environment so that the Test Smart Meter is metering electricity at a measurable rate.

3. Tester shall follow the methods in the Vendor's response to RVI.NEMA-3A.1 to install Image B on the Test Smart Meter.

4. Tester shall confirm that the measurement and storage of Metered Data is not interrupted.

Test Results and Records

1. Tester shall record all Required Vendor Information that was used for the test.

2. Tester shall record all messages, responses, and event log records created during the test.

3. The test passes if all Test Steps complete successfully and Tester was able to positively confirm step 4.

FR.NEMA-9A Initiation of Firmware Upgrade Activation

Reference: NEMA SG-AMI 1-2009, Section 3.2.9

"Smart Meter shall support a mechanism for coordinating activation of Firmware Image updates. Specifically, the Smart Meter shall not activate the new Firmware Image until instructed to do so."

Conditionality:　　　　This Functional Requirement is mandatory for an Upgrade Management System and Smart Meter tested together as a System-Under-Test.

Required Vendor Information

RVI.NEMA-9A.1　　　　Vendor shall document the method for uploading a Firmware Image.

RVI.NEMA-9A.2　　　　Vendor shall document the method for activating a Firmware Upgrade.

RVI.NEMA-9A.3　　　　Vendor shall supply Tester with two firmware images, Image A to be present on the Smart Meter before the upgrade, and Image B to be installed during the upgrade. The response to RVI.NEMA-2A.3 may satisfy this requirement.

Required Test Procedures

RTP.NEMA-9A.1　　　　Tester shall verify that the Activation function is distinct from the firmware upload to the Smart Meter.

Test Steps

1. Tester shall review the Vendor's response to RVI.NEMA-9A.1 and RVI.NEMA-9A.2 and confirm that the method for uploading a Firmware Image is different from the method for activating a Firmware Upgrade.

Test Results and Records

1. Tester shall record all Required Vendor Information that was used for the test.

2. The test passes if all Test Steps complete successfully and Tester was able to positively confirm step 1.

RTP.NEMA-9A.2   Tester shall upload the firmware as documented in the Vendor's response to RVI.NEMA-9A.1 and verify that the firmware upgrade does not take place.

Test Steps

1. Tester shall install Image A on a Test Smart Meter.

2. Tester shall follow the methods in the Vendor's response to RVI.NEMA-9A.1 to upload Image B on the Test Smart Meter.

3. Tester shall invoke the firmware version identification method as documented by the Vendor in response to RVI.NEMA-1A.2 and record the version returned.

4. Tester shall confirm that the version returned matches the version for Image A.

Test Results and Records

1. Tester shall record all Required Vendor Information that was used for the test.

2. Tester shall record all messages, responses, and event log records created during the test.

3. The test passes if all Test Steps complete successfully and Tester was able to positively confirm step 4.

RTP.NEMA-9A.3   Tester shall activate the firmware upgrade as documented in the Vendor's response to RVI.NEMA-9A.2 and verify that the firmware upgrade does take place without the activation function as documented in the Vendor's response to RVI.NEMA-9.1A.

Test Steps

1. Tester shall install Image A on a Test Smart Meter.

2. Tester shall follow the methods in the Vendor's response to RVI.NEMA-9A.1 to upload Image B on the Test Smart Meter.

3. Tester shall follow the methods in the Vendor's response to RVI.NEMA-9A.2 to activate the installation of Image B on the Test Smart Meter.

4. Tester shall invoke the firmware version identification method as documented by the Vendor in response to RVI.NEMA-1A.2 and record the version returned.

5. Tester shall confirm that the version returned matches the version for Image B.

Test Results and Records

1. Tester shall record all Required Vendor Information that was used for the test.

2. Tester shall record all messages, responses, and event log records created during the test.

3. The test passes if all Test Steps complete successfully and Tester was able to positively confirm step 5.

FR.NEMA-10A	Firmware Upgrade Authorization

Reference: NEMA SG-AMI 1-2009, Section 3.2.10

"Smart Meter Upgrade Process shall require authorized initiation."

Conditionality: This Functional Requirement is mandatory for an Upgrade Management System and Smart Meter tested together as a System-Under-Test.

Required Vendor Information

RVI.NEMA-10A.1 Vendor shall document how Firmware Upgrade Authorization is enforced. Documentation shall explain how the authorization process works, including the authentication method and the means to ensure that the authenticated user has authorization to upgrade the firmware.

RVI.NEMA-10A.2 Vendor shall supply Tester with two firmware images, Image A to be present on the Smart Meter before the upgrade, and Image B to be installed during the upgrade. The response to RVI.NEMA-2A.3 may satisfy this requirement.

Required Test Procedures

RTP.NEMA-10A.1 Tester shall verify that the Firmware Upgrade process requires a command from an authorized user, and it completes successfully when an authorized user initiates it.

Test Steps

1. Tester shall install Image A on a Test Smart Meter.

2. Using the credentials of an authorized user as documented in the Vendor's response to RVI.NEMA-10A.1, Tester shall follow the methods in the Vendor's response to RVI.NEMA-3A.1 to install Image B on the Test Smart Meter.

3. Tester shall invoke the firmware version identification function documented in the Vendor's response to RVI.NEMA-1A.2 and record the version returned by the SUT.

4. Tester shall confirm that the version returned matches the version for Image B.

Test Results and Records

1. Tester shall record all Required Vendor Information that was used for the test.

2. Tester shall record all messages, responses, and event log records created during the test.

3. The test passes if all Test Steps complete successfully and Tester was able to positively confirm step 4.

RTP.NEMA-10A.2 Tester shall verify the Firmware Upgrade process fails if initiated by an unauthorized user.

Test Steps

1. Tester shall install Image A on a Test Smart Meter.

2. Using the credentials of an unauthorized user as documented in the Vendor's response to RVI.NEMA-10A.1, Tester shall follow the methods in the Vendor's response to RVI.NEMA-3A.1 to attempt to install Image B on the Test Smart Meter.

3. Tester shall invoke the firmware version identification function documented in the Vendor's response to RVI.NEMA-1A.2 and record the version returned by the SUT.

4. Tester shall confirm that the version returned matches the version for Image A.

Test Results and Records

1. Tester shall record all Required Vendor Information that was used for the test.

2. Tester shall record all messages, responses, and event log records created during the test.

3. The test passes if all Test Steps complete successfully and Tester was able to positively confirm step 4.

RTP.NEMA-10A.3 Tester shall verify the Firmware Upgrade process fails if initiated without authentication.

Test Steps

1. Tester shall install Image A on a Test Smart Meter.

2. If possible, Tester shall follow the methods in the Vendor's response to RVI.NEMA-3A.1 to install Image B on the Test Smart Meter without authenticating as documented in the Vendor's response to RVI.NEMA-10A.1.

3. Tester shall invoke the firmware version identification function documented in the Vendor's response to RVI.NEMA-1A.2 and record the version returned by the SUT.

4. Tester shall confirm that the version returned matches the version for Image B.

Test Results and Records

1. Tester shall record all Required Vendor Information that was used for the test.

2. Tester shall record all messages, responses, and event log records created during the test.

3. The test passes if all Test Steps complete successfully and Tester was able to positively confirm step 4.

FR.NEMA-11A   Firmware Authentication

Reference: NEMA SG-AMI 1-2009, Section 3.2.11

"Smart Meter shall validate that the Firmware Image comes from a trusted source."

Conditionality: This Functional Requirement is mandatory for an Upgrade Management System and Smart Meter tested together as a System-Under-Test.

Required Vendor Information

RVI.NEMA-11A.1　　Vendor shall document how the Smart Meter validates that the Firmware Image comes from a trusted source.

RVI.NEMA-11A.2　　Vendor shall supply Tester with two firmware images, Image A to be present on the Smart Meter before the upgrade, and the untrusted Image D. If digital certificates are used to validate the Firmware Image, "untrusted" means based on certificates that were not issued by trusted keys, expired certificates, and revoked certificates. In this case, Images D1, D2, and D3 shall be produced according to those three scenarios. If another mechanism is used, an Image D shall be produced exhibiting each failure mode in the trust process.

Required Test Procedures

RTP.NEMA-11A.1　　Tester shall examine Image A to verify that data authentication techniques are applied to verify the source of the firmware image Smart Meter as described in the Vendor's response to RVI.NEMA-11A.1.

Test Steps

1. Based on the Vendor's response to RVI.NEMA-11A.1, Tester shall examine the contents of the data authentication portion of examine Image A to confirm that it contains a technique for identifying the source of the firmware image.

Test Results and Records

1. Tester shall record all Required Vendor Information that was used for the test.

2. The test passes if Tester was able to positively confirm step 1.

RTP.NEMA-11A.2　　Tester shall perform the Firmware Upgrade process with each of the D images provided by the vendor in response to RVI.NEMA-11A.2 and verify that the process fails.

Test Steps

1. Tester shall install Image A on a Test Smart Meter.

2. Tester shall follow the methods in the Vendor's response to RVI.NEMA-3A.1 to install Image D1 on the Test Smart Meter.

3. Tester shall invoke the firmware version identification function documented in the Vendor's response to RVI.NEMA-1A.2 and record the version returned by the SUT.

4. Tester shall confirm that the version returned matches the version for Image B.

5. Tester shall repeat these steps for each Image D.

Test Results and Records

1. Tester shall record all Required Vendor Information that was used for the test.

2. Tester shall record all messages, responses, and event log records created during the test.

3. The test passes if all Test Steps complete successfully and Tester was able to positively confirm step 4.

FR.NEMA-12A   Cryptographic Algorithms

Reference: NEMA SG-AMI 1-2009, Section 4.1

"Cryptographic algorithms shall be current, publically vetted, and government-approved."

Conditionality: This Functional Requirement is mandatory for an Upgrade Management System and Smart Meter tested together as a System-Under-Test.

Required Vendor Information

RVI.NEMA-12A.1   Vendor shall list all cryptographic algorithms supported by the Smart Meter under test. If the Smart Meter uses a cryptographic module validated for conformance to FIPS 140-2[10] [FIPS 140] or later, the cryptographic module's Security Policy will suffice to meet this requirement. If the Smart Meter uses cryptographic algorithms that have been validated by the Cryptographic Algorithm Validation Program[11] or by other recognized authority, vendor shall provide proof of validation.

Required Test Procedures

RTP.NEMA-12A.1   Tester shall determine whether the cryptographic algorithms used are current, publicly vetted, and government-approved.

Test Steps

1. Tester shall confirm that all cryptographic algorithms identified in the Vendor's response to RVI.NEMA-12.1 are government-approved. In the United States, government-approved algorithms are those included in NIST's Computer Security Resource Center's Cryptographic Algorithm Validation Program. Note that validation of the algorithm implementations or cryptographic modules is not required by the standard.

Test Results and Records

1. Tester shall record all Required Vendor Information that was used for the test.

2. The test passes if all Test Steps complete successfully and Tester was able to positively confirm step 1.

FR.NEMA-13A   Cryptography Strengths

Reference: NEMA SG-AMI 1-2009, Section 4.2

"Cryptography strengths shall support Smart Meters deployed toward the end of a product's life cycle and be designed to provide a useful twenty-year service life—at a minimum, those cryptography strength time spans noted in NIST Special Publication SP 800-57, Part 1 (revised March 2007)."

---

[10] http://csrc.nist.gov/groups/STM/cmvp/index.html
[11] http://csrc.nist.gov/groups/STM/cavp/index.html

Conditionality: This Functional Requirement is mandatory for an Upgrade Management System and Smart Meter tested together as a System-Under-Test.

Required Vendor Information

RVI.NEMA-13A.1   Vendor shall list all the key sizes used by the cryptographic algorithms.

Required Test Procedures

RTP.NEMA-13A.1   Tester shall determine if the strengths identified by the vendor comply with a twenty-year duration cryptography strength time spans according the document cited in the requirement.

Test Steps

1. NIST Special Publication SP 800-57 Part 1 Table 3 identifies 128 bits of key strength as necessary for a twenty-year security life for keys generated 2011 or later.

2. Tester shall refer to NIST Special Publication SP 800-57 Part 1 Table 2 to confirm that all key sizes identified in the Vendor's response to RVI.NEMA-13A.1 provide 128 or more bits of security.

Test Results and Records

1. Tester shall record all Required Vendor Information that was used for the test.

2. The test passes if all Test Steps complete successfully and Tester was able to positively confirm step 2.

FR.NEMA-14A   Resilient AMI System Design

Reference: NEMA SG-AMI 1-2009, Section 4.3

"AMI system design shall ensure that compromise of a single Smart Meter does not lead to compromise of the AMI system at large."

Conditionality: It is mandatory for an Upgrade Management System and Smart Meter tested together as a System-Under-Test to support this AMI system design requirement.

Required Vendor Information

RVI.NEMA-14A.1   Vendor shall document the mechanisms that ensure that the Smart Meters in an AMI system do not use the same passwords and keys when operational. This could be accomplished by generating unique initial passwords and keys for all Smart Meters, or by requiring a change of passwords and keys during system configuration. If the Smart Meter enforces such a change of passwords and keys before operating, vendor documentation shall explain that process.

Required Test Procedures

RTP.NEMA-14A.1   Tester shall verify that a Smart Meter that has been configured according to Vendor guidance does not share default passwords or keys.

Test Steps

1. Tester shall follow the procedures documented in RVI.NEMA-14A.1 to install and configure a Test Smart Meter.

2. Tester shall verify that all passwords and keys used by the SUT have been randomly generated or generated by the Tester during the installation and configuration process.

Test Results and Records

1. Tester shall record all Required Vendor Information that was used for the test.

2. The test passes if all Test Steps complete successfully and Tester was able to positively confirm step 2.

FR.NEMA-15A   Authentication and Integrity of Command Messages

Reference: NEMA SG-AMI 1-2009, Section 4.4

"Security protections shall provide strong authentication and integrity mechanisms to ensure that command messages to and from Smart Meters are not altered in transit or forged."

Conditionality: This Functional Requirement is mandatory for an Upgrade Management System and Smart Meter tested together as a System-Under-Test.

Required Vendor Information

RVI.NEMA-15A.1   Vendor shall document what security protections the SUT provides for command messages.

Required Test Procedures

RTP.NEMA-15A.1   If the SUT provides security protections for command messages, Tester shall confirm that the authentication and integrity mechanisms are in place.

Test Steps

1. Tester shall attempt to issue commands to the SUT using incorrect authentication credentials, and verify that the commands fail and the authentication errors are logged.

2. Tester shall attempt to issue commands with the integrity mechanism subverted, and verify that the commands fail and the integrity errors are logged.

Test Results and Records

1. Tester shall record all Required Vendor Information that was used for the test.

2. The test passes if all Test Steps complete successfully and Tester was able to positively confirm steps 1 and 2.

RTP.NEMA-15A.2   If SUT relies on another component to provide security protections for command messages, clearly indicate this in the Test Report.

FR.NEMA-16A   Security Protections on Firmware Upgrade and Disconnect

Reference: NEMA SG-AMI 1-2009, Section 4.5

"Security protections shall extend to all field operation commands within the Smart Meter, with particular attention to operating the disconnect switch and modifying the device Firmware Image."

Conditionality: This Functional Requirement is mandatory for an Upgrade Management System and Smart Meter tested together as a System-Under-Test.

Required Vendor Information

RVI.NEMA-16A.1   Vendor shall document all security protections on field operation commands within the Smart Meter.

Required Test Procedures

RTP.NEMA-16A.1   If the SUT provides security protections on field operation commands, Tester shall confirm that security protections apply to remote disconnect and firmware upgrade functions.

Test Steps

1. Tester shall follow the vendor's instructions to initiate a firmware upgrade.

2. Tester shall verify that the security protections identified in RVI.NEMA-16A.1 are required to perform the firmware upgrade.

3. If the Test Smart Meter supports a remote disconnect capability, Tester shall follow the vendor's instructions to initiate the remote disconnect.

4. Tester shall verify that the security protections identified in RVI.NEMA-16A.1 are required to perform the remote disconnect.

Test Results and Records

1. Tester shall record all Required Vendor Information that was used for the test.

2. The test passes if all Test Steps complete successfully and Tester was able to positively confirm steps 2 and 4.

RTP.NEMA-16A.2   If the SUT relies on another component to provide security protections on field operation commands, Tester shall clearly indicate this in the Test Report.

FR.NEMA-18A   Forgery Protection

Reference: NEMA SG-AMI 1-2009, Section 4.7

"Security protections shall provide protection against forgery of Smart Meter data."

Conditionality: This Functional Requirement is mandatory for an Upgrade Management System and Smart Meter tested together as a System-Under-Test.

Required Vendor Information

RVI.NEMA-18A.1   Vendor shall document all security protections provided by the Smart Meter that protect against forgery of Smart Meter data.

Required Test Procedures

RTP.NEMA-18A.1   If the SUT provides security protections against forgery of Smart Meter data, Tester shall confirm that security protections identified in the Vendor's response to RVI.NEMA-18A.1 work properly.

Test Steps

1. Tester shall verify that the security protections listed in RVI.NEMA-18A.1 are in place.

Test Results and Records

1. Tester shall record all Required Vendor Information that was used for the test.

2. The test passes if all Test Steps complete successfully and Tester was able to positively confirm step 1.

RTP.NEMA-18A.2   If the SUT relies on another component to provide security protections against forgery of Smart Meter data, Tester shall clearly indicate this in the Test Report.

FR.NEMA-19A   Defense In Depth from HAN

Reference: NEMA SG-AMI 1-2009, Section 4.8

"AMI systems shall employ a defense-in-depth strategy that shields Smart Grid Communication Networks from Home Area Networks."

Conditionality: It is mandatory for an Upgrade Management System and Smart Meter tested together as a System-Under-Test to support this AMI system design requirement.

Required Vendor Information

RVI.NEMA-19A.1   Vendor shall document all measures the Smart Meter takes to shield the Smart Grid Communication Networks from Home Area Networks.

Required Test Procedures

RTP.NEMA-19A.1   Tester shall confirm that security protections identified in the Vendor's response to RVI.NEMA-19A.1 work properly.

Test Steps

1. Tester shall verify that the security protections listed in RVI.NEMA-19A.1 are in place.

Test Results and Records

1. Tester shall record all Required Vendor Information that was used for the test.

2. The test passes if all Test Steps complete successfully and Tester was able to positively confirm step 1.

FR.NEMA-20A   Intrusion Detection

Reference: NEMA SG-AMI 1-2009, Section 4.9

"AMI systems shall support anomaly and/or intrusion detection that indicate that Smart Meters may have been compromised, or when abnormal activity is detected."

Conditionality: It is mandatory for an Upgrade Management System and Smart Meter tested together as a System-Under-Test to support this AMI system design requirement.

Required Vendor Information

RVI.NEMA-20A.1   Vendor shall document how the SUT supports a systematic anomaly and/or intrusion detection capability, including what conditions are detected and what alarms or messages are generated in response.

Required Test Procedures

RTP.NEMA-20A.1   Tester shall verify that the functions the SUT implements in support of a systematic intrusion detection capability work as documented in the Vendor's response to RVI.NEMA-20A.1.

Test Steps

1. Tester shall attempt to trigger the intrusion detection mechanism, and verify that the expected alarms or messages are generated in response.

Test Results and Records

1. Tester shall record all Required Vendor Information that was used for the test.

2. The test passes if all Test Steps complete successfully and Tester was able to positively confirm step 1.

FR.NEMA-21A   Log Authentication and Encryption Failures

Reference: NEMA SG-AMI 1-2009, Section 4.10

"Logging and auditing mechanism shall be in place to show when authentication or encrypted communications fail."

Conditionality: This Functional Requirement is mandatory for an Upgrade Management System and Smart Meter tested together as a System-Under-Test.

Required Vendor Information

RVI.NEMA-21A.1   Vendor shall document the technique by which authentication failures are logged.

RVI.NEMA-21A.2   Vendor shall document the technique by which encrypted communications failures are logged.

Required Test Procedures

RTP.NEMA-21A.1   RVI.NEMA-15A.1 step 1 verifies that authentication failures are logged.

RTP.NEMA-21A.2   Tester shall verify the technique by which encrypted communications failures are logged, and test the correct implementation of the auditing mechanism and that the data logged is accurate and complete.

Test Steps

1. Test step 1 of RTP.NEMA-15A.1 verifies that authentication failures are logged.
2. Tester shall induce a failure of encrypted communications and verify that the failure is logged.

Test Results and Records

1. Tester shall record all Required Vendor Information that was used for the test.
2. The test passes if all Test Steps complete successfully and Tester was able to positively confirm step 1 and 2.

A.3 Conformance Tests for Conditional Requirements for SUT

The following Functional Requirements are mandatory when certain conditions are met. The requirements are excluded from the Mandatory Conformance Test Requirements (Section A.2) either because i) they require security protections that can be provided by the Upgrade Management System and Smart Meter together or by the AMI Network; or ii) the Smart Meter can choose from multiple ways to meet a mandatory requirement. If a Smart Meter vendor implements these requirements within the Upgrade Management System and Smart Meter, then to demonstrate conformance to these requirements, they shall use the methods below.

FR.NEMA-2Aa   **Firmware Upgrade Recovery to Previously Installed Firmware**

Reference: NEMA SG-AMI 1-2009, Section 3.2.2

"Smart Meter shall recover to the previously installed Firmware … if unable to complete the Upgrade Process."

Conditionality: This Functional Requirement is mandatory for an Upgrade Management System and Smart Meter tested together as a System-Under-Test that recovers to previously installed Firmware, according to the Vendor's response to RVI.NEMA-2A.1.

Required Vendor Information

RVI.NEMA-2Aa.1   Vendor shall document the process by which the Smart Meter recovers to the previously installed Firmware.

RVI.NEMA-2Aa.2   Vendor shall supply Tester with two firmware images, Image A to be present on the Smart Meter before the upgrade, and Image B to be installed during the upgrade. The response to RVI.NEMA-2A.3 may satisfy this requirement.

Required Test Procedures

RTP.NEMA-2Aa.1   Tester shall induce a failure in the firmware upgrade process and verify that the Smart Meter recovers to the previously installed firmware (using the firmware version identification function documented in the Vendor's response to RVI.NEMA-1A.1).

Test Steps

1. Tester shall install Image A on a Test Smart Meter.

2. Tester shall follow the methods in the Vendor's response to RVI.NEMA-3A.1 to initiate the installation of Image B on the Test Smart Meter.

3. Tester shall induce a failure in the installation process.

4. Tester shall invoke the firmware version identification function documented in the Vendor's response to RVI.NEMA-1A.2 and record the version returned by the SUT.

5. Tester shall confirm that the version returned matches the version for Image A.

Test Results and Records

1. Tester shall record all Required Vendor Information that was used for the test.

2. Tester shall record all messages, responses, and event log records created during the test.

3. The test passes if all Test Steps complete successfully and Tester was able to positively confirm step 5.

FR.NEMA-2Ab   Firmware Upgrade Recovery Failed Upgrade Process Alarm

Reference: NEMA SG-AMI 1-2009, Section 3.2.2

"Smart Meter shall ... initiate a 'Failed Upgrade Process' alarm to the Network Management System or the Upgrade Management System if unable to complete the Upgrade Process."

Conditionality: This Functional Requirement is mandatory for an Upgrade Management System and Smart Meter tested together as a System-Under-Test that initiates a "Failed Upgrade Process" alarm according to the Vendor's response to RVI.NEMA-2A.1.

Required Vendor Information

RVI.NEMA-2Ab.1   Vendor shall document how to identify the Failed Upgrade Process alarm (i.e., where the alarm is sent, the alarm properties, etc.).

RVI.NEMA-2Ab.2   Vendor shall supply Tester with two firmware images, Image A to be present on the Smart Meter before the upgrade, and Image B to be installed during the upgrade. The response to RVI.NEMA-2A.3 may satisfy this requirement.

Required Test Procedures

RTP.NEMA-2Ab.1   Tester shall induce a failure in the upgrade process and verify that the Smart Meter sends an alarm as described in the Vendor's response to RVI.NEMA-2Ab.1.

Test Steps

1. Tester shall install Image A on a Test Smart Meter.

2. Tester shall follow the methods in the Vendor's response to RVI.NEMA-3A.1 to initiate the installation of Image B on the Test Smart Meter.

3. Tester shall induce a failure in the installation process.

4. Tester shall confirm that a Failed Upgrade Process alarm is sent as specified in the vendor response to RVI.NEMA-2Ab.1.

Test Results and Records

1. Tester shall record all Required Vendor Information that was used for the test.

2. Tester shall record all messages, responses, and event log records created during the test.

3. The test passes if all Test Steps complete successfully and Tester was able to positively confirm step 4.

A.4   Conformance Tests for Optional Requirements for SUT

The following Functional Requirements are excluded from the mandatory Conformance Test Requirements (Section A.2) because they pertain to optional functional requirements in the Standard. If a Smart Meter vendor implements these requirements within the Upgrade Management System and Smart Meter tested as a single System-Under-Test, then they may use the methods below to demonstrate conformance to these requirements.

FR.NEMA-2Ac	Firmware Upgrade Recovery Safe Inactive Mode

Reference: NEMA SG-AMI 1-2009, Section 3.2.2

"… if the Smart Meter has detected a hardware failure during the Upgrade Process (such as failed Electrically-Erasable Read Only Memory, or EEROM), the Smart Meter may alternatively enter into a safe inactive mode."

Conditionality: This Functional Requirement is optional for an Upgrade Management System and Smart Meter tested together as a System-Under-Test. An Upgrade Management System and Smart Meter tested together as a System-Under-Test that supports an inactive mode upon hardware failure may incorporate this Functional Requirement.

Required Vendor Information

RVI.NEMA-2Ac.1   Vendor shall document how the Smart Meter enters and recovers from the safe inactive mode.

RVI.NEMA-2Ac.2   Vendor shall supply Tester with two firmware images, Image A to be present on the Smart Meter before the upgrade, and Image B to be installed during the upgrade. The response to RVI.NEMA-2A.3 may satisfy this requirement.

Required Test Procedures

RTP.NEMA-2Ac.1   Tester shall induce a hardware failure in the firmware upgrade process and verify that the Smart Meter enters an inactive mode.

Test Steps

1. Tester shall install Image A on a Test Smart Meter.

2. Tester shall follow the methods in the Vendor's response to RVI.NEMA-3A.1 to initiate the installation of Image B on the Test Smart Meter.

3. Tester shall induce a failure in the installation process.

63

4. Tester shall verify that the meter enters the safe inactive mode as documented in the vendor response to RVI.NEMA-2Ac.1.

Test Results and Records

1. Tester shall record all Required Vendor Information that was used for the test.

2. Tester shall record all messages, responses, and event log records created during the test.

3. The test passes if all Test Steps complete successfully and Tester was able to positively confirm step 4.

Annex B – References

[NEMA]   National Electrical Manufacturers Association Smart Grid Standards Publication SG-AMI 1-2009, *Requirements for Smart Meter Upgradeability*, 2009.

[FIPS-140]   National Institute of Standards and Technology, FIPS 140-2, *Security Requirements for Cryptographic Modules*, 2001 or latest, http://csrc.nist.gov/publications/PubsFIPS.html

[SP800-57]   National Institute of Standards and Technology, SP 800-57 Part 1, *Recommendation for Key Management: Part 1: General*, 2012 or latest, http://csrc.nist.gov/publications/PubsSPs.html

www.ingramcontent.com/pod-product-compliance
Lightning Source LLC
Chambersburg PA
CBHW060459060326
40689CB00020B/4592